Kni

20 WITHDRAWN

Knitting
200 Q&A

Questions answered on everything
from casting on to decorative effects

Rita Taylor

BARRON'S

A QUANTUM BOOK

First edition for the United States, its territories and possessions,
and Canada published in 2008 by Barron's Educational Series, Inc.

All inquiries should be addressed to:
Barron's Educational Series, Inc.
250 Wireless Boulevard
Hauppauge, New York 11788
www.barronseduc.com

The Library of Congress has catalogued the hardcover edition as follows:

ISBN-10: 0-7641-6137-7
ISBN-13: 978-0-7641-6137-7

Library of Congress Control Number: 2007937130

This book is published and produced by
Quantum Books
6 Blundell Street
London N7 9BH

QUM2KQ2

Manufactured in Singapore by Pica Digital Pte Ltd.
Printed in China by CT Printing Limited

9 8 7 6 5 4 3 2 1

Designers: e-Digital Design
Design Consultant: Richard Dewing
Photographer: Philip Wilkins
Hand Model: Amy Hardingham
Project Editor: Derek Hall
Managing Editor: Jimmy Topham
Publisher: Anastasia Cavouras

All images are the copyright of Quantum Publishing, except for the following,
which are copyright Knit Today – p149: issue no. 9 May 2007;
p169: issue no. 12 August 2007; p207: issue no. 12 August 2007.

CONTENTS

INTRODUCTION

Knitting has an elusive history, although it seems certain that it originated in the Far East, perhaps in the eleventh century. There are very few ancient pieces of the craft in existence, and those originally thought to have been knitted were later discovered to have been produced by a similar technique known as nalbinding. Early pieces of knitting were probably produced for purely practical reasons; as they wore out they were discarded. They were made from perishable fibers and thus there are only fragments of fabric to study—no whole pieces—which also makes it difficult to discern exactly how they were constructed.

The pieces that can be authenticated were usually made for special occasions, especially religious ceremonies, and they are fine examples of the craft. Craftsmen belonging to the artisans' guilds also made other pieces that have been preserved. Items had to be made following specific instructions— for example, stockings were to be decorated with "clocks," a form of fine cabling, and a knitted beret had to be felted. But the main piece an apprentice was required to make before becoming a master was a knitted carpet containing at least a dozen colors; this was probably intended as a wall hanging.

Very few "everyday" pieces of knitting produced before the twentieth century have been preserved. However, there are some items from the nineteenth and early twentieth centuries that show very high levels of craftsmanship. Fortunately many of these have survived, since it was probably intended that they would be passed on to the next generation. Christening shawls and robes are examples of items that come into this category. Many more knitted items are preserved today, as we realize the importance of retaining them as part of our heritage.

There were no written instructions for knitters to follow until the nineteenth century. Early knitters learned by observation and word of mouth; if we study some of the early pieces we may be able to discover some part of what was once common knowledge. As well as demonstrating the skills of the designer and worker (the same person in most cases), this work also reveals techniques that may have been forgotten or lost.

In writing this book I have tried to pass on some of the techniques that I have learned over many years and to demystify some of the terms used. Knitting language can be inhibiting to a beginner, and having to follow instructions to the letter prevents many people from taking up the craft. However, the methods described are not rules to be followed rigidly but simply descriptions of the way different techniques are worked. Various methods of working have been developed over the years, and if you watch how the stitches perform as you manipulate them you will gain the confidence to try out ideas of your own.

This book is aimed at knitters with all levels of experience. For those who are new to knitting, it begins with an explanation of how to get started, including a brief guide to the types of yarns and needles available. The first stage of knitting, casting on, is described, and this is followed by illustrations of the less well known types of cast-on and the ways in which they can be used in order to achieve the most appropriate and satisfactory appearance. The next chapter explains how to work the two basic stitches, knit and purl, and how to combine these to form various patterns. This is followed by descriptions of the different ways of binding off, giving you all the knowledge you need to complete your first piece of knitting.

When you have mastered these techniques you will want to progress to more adventurous types of knitting. Where appropriate, more than one method of working is described, to encourage knitters to break away from rigid pattern instructions and choose techniques to suit themselves. In the chapters that follow you will find advice on different methods

of increasing and decreasing, working with circular needles, and tackling what is often referred to as the more advanced range of techniques such as color work, cables, and lace. I hope that the advice given will show that these types of knitting are no more difficult than working a plain garment. In addition, you will experience a real sense of achievement when a more challenging piece of work is finished.

Once the knitting is completed, the pieces must be joined together and the ways of doing this are described, along with advice on picking up stitches and creating various kinds of buttonholes. Toward the end of the book there are more hints and tips gleaned from years of knitting, plus others provided by friends and fellow knitters, and there is also a section on freeform and other kinds of decorative knitting. Armed with this technical information it is just a short step to creating your own designs, and there is some advice on devising and using charts for this purpose.

Whether you are a beginner or a knitter with several years of experience, I hope that this book will encourage you to practice, experiment, discover, and create. Knitting is a wonderful craft, at whichever level you practice it. It is not only immensely satisfying but it also encourages us to use our imaginations.

1 TOOLS AND MATERIALS

Yarn and needles are really all you need for getting started, but the more you know about them the better. This chapter also explains some common technical terms.

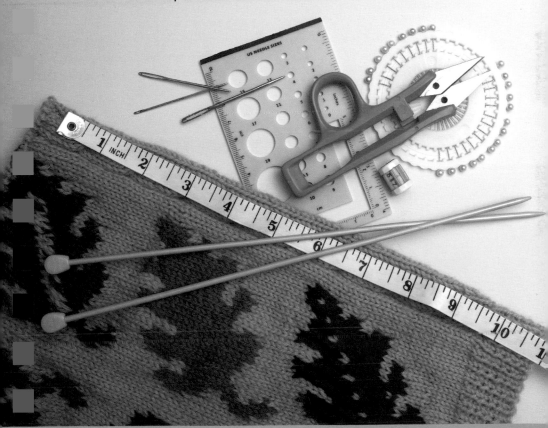

Question 1:
What is yarn?

Strictly speaking, yarn is knitting material made from fibers—either natural or synthetic—that have been spun together. Today, however, all kinds of fibers are referred to as yarn, whether they are woven, cut into strips, or extruded. You can even make your own yarns from strips of fabric or plastic sewn or knotted together. So long as you can form a continuous length of the material, you can knit with it.

Yarn can be spun into various textures, and new techniques constantly evolve to produce different effects. Yarn also comes in different thicknesses, the most usual being fingering, sportweight, worsted, and bulky. Synthetics, being lighter in weight than most natural fibers, are often spun into even thicker yarn.

Yarn that is ready to knit may be supplied as balls, skeins, spools, or cones and will usually carry a label describing its fiber content, weight, length, and suggested needle size for a given gauge.

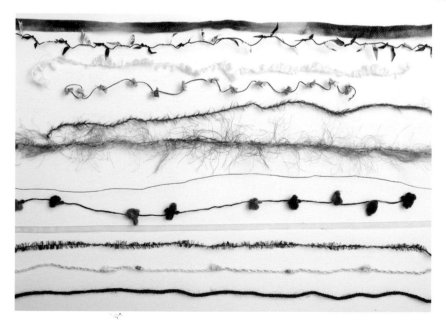

Question 2:
Which is the best yarn?

The best yarn is the one suited to its particular purpose. You would not want to make a baby's blanket from harsh, synthetic fiber, but neither would you choose to make a shopping bag with the finest one-ply fingering wool!

Sometimes the yarn itself is an inspiration for a design, but do check the fiber's properties on the ball band before going ahead and making something for which it is not suited. As a general rule, an item that is highly patterned works best in a smooth yarn that will show the stitches to best advantage, whereas a plain garment can be worked in a much wider variety of yarns, such as slubby, boucle, or brushed, and each type will give a totally different effect.

However, for many people wool is the favored knitting yarn. As well as being excellent to knit with and to wear, it comes in a wide variety of thicknesses and colors. At the "luxury" end of the scale there are also alpaca, silk, and cashmere, and various combinations of these mixed with other fibers.

Question 3:
How do I hold the yarn?

There are various ways to hold the yarn, but the most common methods are those called English and Continental. The first method usually involves holding the yarn in the right hand, winding it around the little finger, over the next two fingers, and around the index finger. The right-hand needle rests between thumb and index finger, and the yarn is manipulated with the index finger.

In the Continental method, the yarn is held in the left hand, wrapped around the little finger, under the next two fingers, and over the index finger from where the yarn is picked up by the tip of the right needle. The needles are held on top.

Left-handed knitters sometimes work using a combination of these two methods.

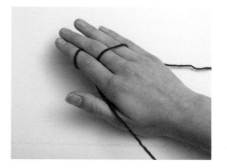

ABOVE English method.

BELOW Continental method.

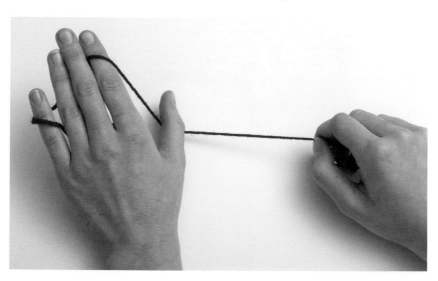

Question 4:
What does "ply" mean?

A ply is actually a layer, which in the case of yarn is usually a strand. A strand is the initial single, twisted thread obtained after the fiber has been spun, and several of these strands are then folded or twisted together again to form the finished yarn. This process is known as "plying."

The more plys there are the thicker the yarn will be, but the number of plys does not indicate the finished thickness; two single strands of a thick thread can be spun together to form a very thick two-ply. You can ply your own yarn by knitting with several strands at once—there is no need to twist it together first. If you are using one of these multi-plyed yarns for a garment remember to choose yarns that have the same washing properties, or wash in accordance with the instructions for the most delicate one.

Question 5:
Why are some two-ply yarns thicker than others?

As already mentioned, there are many different ways of producing yarn. Each individual thread can be spun to any thickness. Subsequently, the fibers can be twisted tightly or firmly, and two-plys twisted together lightly will give a thicker-looking finished product than those that are twisted tightly together. Many Shetland yarns are twisted lightly, and their two-ply yarns are as thick as sportweight. The weight of the fiber itself can also affect the thickness of the finished product, as can the dye that is used.

Terms such as "two-ply" or "four-ply" do not indicate the thickness of the yarn but simply indicate how many strands have been twisted together to form that particular yarn.

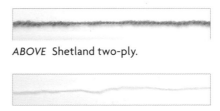

ABOVE Shetland two-ply.

ABOVE Merino two-ply.

Question 6:
What are "Z twist" and "S twist"?

The initial twist of the yarn is achieved in the spinning and depends on the direction of the wheel. It usually produces a Z twist that is, when you view the yarn sideways on, the fibers appear to follow the shape of a letter Z. So that the yarn will not twist back on itself as it does when you make a twisted cord, it must be plied in the opposite direction to that in which it was spun—in other words, with an S twist.

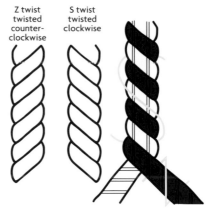

Z twist
twisted
counter-
clockwise

S twist
twisted
clockwise

S twist and Z twist
plied together to form
S twist knitting yarn

Question 7:
Which are the best needles?

The best needles are those that do not hinder your speed and are pleasant and comfortable to use. There are many different types of needle available nowadays; even some with lights on the end so that you can knit in the dark! They range in size from fine needles for miniature knitting to huge, custom-made needles of whatever size you can manage to hold for multistrand, "extreme" knitting!

The most common U.S. needle sizes, beginning with the finest, range from 0 upward. The numbers indicate the circumference of the needle, from 0.08 inches (2 mm) to 0.4 inches (10 mm). Needles also come in different lengths—from 6 inches (15 cm) to about 16 inches (40.5 cm) for the main range of sizes.

Needles are available in various materials, such as metal, bamboo, wood, and plastic or other synthetics, and are usually of uniform thickness along their length apart from the points. These needles come in pairs, have a knob at one end, and are often referred to as straights or single-points. They are used for all kinds of flat knitting, and the smoother they are, the better the stitches will slide along the shaft.

Circular knitting, or knitting in the round, is carried out with sets of double-pointed needles or circular needles. Double-pointed needles are sold in sets of four or five, and are also made from different kinds of materials. Circular needles usually consist of two short pointed ends joined with a flexible cord. These are also sold in different lengths to accommodate the number of stitches; it is better to have a lot of stitches on a short needle rather than try to stretch a few stitches around a long one. However, very short circulars can be awkward to use, and it is often better to use double-pointed needles for small numbers of stitches.

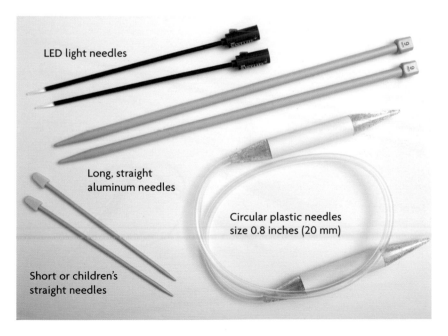

LED light needles

Long, straight
aluminum needles

Circular plastic needles
size 0.8 inches (20 mm)

Short or children's
straight needles

Question 10:
What should I do if I find a knot in the yarn?

It is never a good idea to leave a knot and hope that it will stay on the wrong side; even if it does, it makes an uneven stitch. If you haven't worked very far along the row, undo your work back to the beginning of that row, undo the knot and then, leaving about 4 or 5 inches (10–13 cm) of yarn, start again. Tie a loose knot and then darn in the ends along the seam at the finish.

If you feel that you have gone too far along the row, undo the knot and knit eight to ten alternate stitches with the new and the old yarn, leaving about 4 inches (10 cm) of each end to darn in later. Alternatively, some yarns can be spliced together by overlapping their ends and twisting them together. Knit with this twisted portion of the yarn carefully, making sure that it does not untwist. Trim off any loose ends when the piece is finished.

If you find several knots in your yarn return it to the supplier with a cover letter, or take it back to your yarn store.

Question 11:
Will I have enough yarn to finish a row?

Make a loose knot or a slipknot one-quarter of the way along the remaining yarn. Knit one-quarter of the stitches in the row, and if you have still not reached the knot you will have enough yarn for the rest of the row.

However, if you can plan ahead, it is better to do the check when there is still enough yarn for two rows. Tie the knot halfway along the yarn and if you haven't reached the knot by the end of the first row, there will be enough for a second one.

Question 12:
What is a cable needle?

Cable needles are short, double-pointed needles that are used to hold stitches temporarily in order to change their position in the row. They come in various thicknesses, and you should use the one closest to the size of needles you are using or one slightly thinner so that the stitches are not stretched too much. Whether you use a straight cable needle or a kinked one is really a matter of personal preference.

BELOW **Curved cable needle holding stitches ready for crossing.**

Question 13:
What is the difference between "rainbow," "space-dyed," and variegated yarns?

All of the above terms are virtually interchangeable, although rainbow is a term less often used these days. There are also yarns described as self-striping, hand-painted, and ombré.

All of these yarns contain a mix of colors applied in various lengths, sometimes, as with self-striping yarns, to deliberately create a pattern over a specific number of stitches. Others are dyed as single strands that are spun together in different directions so that no two balls of yarn are ever exactly the same. Most hand-painted yarns are dyed so that they also produce totally random and unpredictable effects. Ombré yarns are sometimes double dyed in parts so that they shade gradually from dark to light and back again.

When joining on new balls of all of these yarns take care that you maintain the sequence of colors and don't start a new ball where there is too great a contrast.

ABOVE Variegated wool.

ABOVE Space-dyed wool.

ABOVE Hand-painted silk.

Question 14:
How can I prevent unwanted patterns from forming with multicolored yarns?

If you find that large, diamond-shaped blocks are forming with some of the space-dyed yarns, use two balls at once and work two rows from each ball in imaginary stripes. However, some yarns, notably those produced for knitting socks, are deliberately dyed in a way that will create stripes, sometimes alternated with a few rows of speckled patterning. The pattern is determined by the number of stitches on the needles and, at the moment, they only work for small items. However, it would be interesting to experiment with one of these yarns on an adult-sized garment worked in the round!

Some yarns, for example Twilley's "Freedom Spirit," are deliberately created to avoid unwanted patterns forming. Two ends, each of which contains four colors, are randomly space-dyed and then spun together. Even if you followed the same pattern again, using the same shade, the garment would come out differently.

BELOW Zig-zag patterns appearing at random.

Question 15:
What is "gauge" or "tension"?

Gauge determines the finished measurements of the piece you are making. If you are following a pattern it is important to achieve the same gauge as that stated, as even one-quarter of a stitch to the inch will make a difference of 2 inches (5 cm) or more across the whole width.

Always make a gauge swatch before starting to knit even when using the recommended yarn, as different dyes can also cause a change in the thickness of a yarn. Change the size of the needles you are using; each change in size will be about one-half a stitch different. Don't simply try to pull the yarn more tightly, as you won't be able to maintain this throughout the piece. The yarn should run freely through your fingers as you knit, and you should feel relaxed and comfortable. The size of needles that you use is not important to the finished piece; the crucial point is that you achieve the same number of stitches and rows as the designer.

If you are designing your own work you will need to know the gauge in order to work out the number of stitches to cast on and the number of rows to knit. Make a few samples on different size needles,

select the sample that gives you the most pleasing effect, and count the number of stitches and rows to 4 inches (10 cm). Divide these figures by four to give you the numbers for 1 inch (2.5 cm), and use these figures to work out your required measurements.

BELOW **This yarn has been knitted with three different needle sizes (US 6, 8, and 10) to demonstrate the effect this has on the gauge.**

Question 16:
What stitch should I use for my gauge?

Sometimes a pattern will tell you to work your gauge in stockinette, even though the piece is highly patterned. This is because it is quite often difficult to measure gauge over a patterned piece.

If the pattern does not give these instructions, or if you are designing a piece of your own, then work the gauge in the main pattern stitch. This is especially true for lace patterns, which "open out" much more than stockinette, and for patterns where

more than one color is used in a row. If you are stranding or weaving in the yarns across the whole row, there will not be as much widthways stretch in the piece as there will be if you are working in one color.

However, if you are working individual motifs by simply twisting the yarns together at the changeover, there will be no pulling of the yarn across the back and the tension will be closer to that of plain stockinette.

Question 17:
How do I measure my gauge swatch?

First of all, make sure that you work a sample large enough to measure. If the pattern states the number of stitches and rows to 4 inches (10 cm) then you need to make a piece at least 5 inches (13 cm) square in order to measure out the required amount. If you want to try out more than one sample, knit one row in a contrast color before changing needles.

When you have finished your swatch, bind off the stitches and block or press the piece as stated on the ball band. Lay it on a flat surface and place a rigid ruler (tape measures can stretch) horizontally across the center. Do not start counting from the edge, since these stitches can be distorted; instead begin two or three stitches in, and then count how many stitches you have in 4 inches (10 cm), including any quarter or half stitches (especially when using a thick yarn). Now do the same with the rows, measuring a few rows up from the cast-on edge. Again, include any fractions of rows, but it is not quite so important to achieve the correct row gauge unless the number of rows is crucial to the stitch pattern.

An alternative method, especially when working a complex pattern

where it is difficult to count the stitches, is to place a marker at the beginning and end of each pattern and measure the width and length between the markers. If it is less than the measurement stated in the pattern then you will need to use larger needles. If it is more, then use smaller ones.

Remember, bigger needles make bigger stitches!

EXPERT TIP

❝If you are working a complicated pattern for a design of your own, then you need to make at least one pattern repeat in your swatch and measure the size of this repeat. You will know the number of stitches in each repeat, so you can then calculate the number of stitches that you will need for your required measurements. ❞

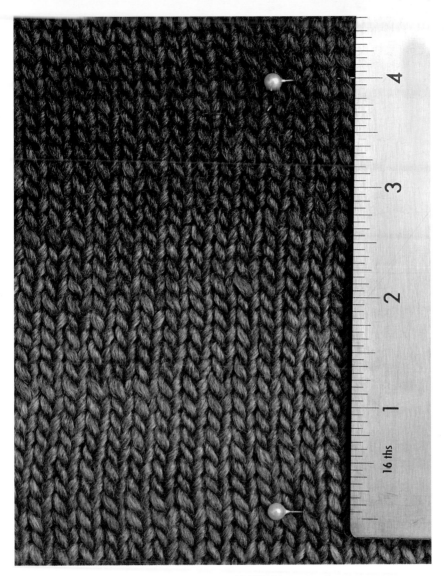

ABOVE Measuring the row gauge between marker pins.

Question 18:
If I change needle size for the main part do I also need to change it for the ribbing?

The simple answer to this is "yes," but the final decision lies with you. If there is only a short length of ribbing at the hem and cuffs the final measurement will not be altered too drastically if you keep to the size stated in the pattern, and you have only changed up or down one size of needle for the main part. But you may feel that you would prefer the ribbing to be a little tighter, in which case use needles one or two sizes smaller.

Question 19:
Approximately how much yarn will I need for a woman's sweater?

If you are following a pattern, it will tell you how much yarn you will need of a specific brand. If you are substituting yarn, or designing your own garment, you will have to make a good estimate of the quantity required. There are two ways you can do this. You can knit one ball and measure the piece obtained with it, then work out the area of the finished garment and thus estimate the number of balls you think you will need altogether. Or, you can knit a measured number of inches of yarn, check the ball band for its length, and work out how many linear inches (in other words, rows) you will need in the whole piece.

As a rough guide, a lightly spun synthetic yarn will go almost twice as far as wool of an equivalent weight, and wool or wool mix yarn will go further than cotton.

RIGHT A cotton cardigan will weigh more than one knitted in wool.

2 CASTING ON

The initial row of loops on the needle is called the
cast-on row. Several methods of casting on are described on
the following pages, each suited to a different purpose.

Question 20:
How do I cast on?

There are several methods of casting on, but the most common are the knitted cast-on, the cable cast-on, and the thumb cast-on. Virtually all cast-ons require you to make a slipknot before you begin. This is done by making a loop in the yarn, drawing the long end of the yarn through this loop, and pulling the other end to draw it up. Place the resulting loop on the needle and pull the long end to fasten it; this slipknot is your first stitch.

Knitted cast-on

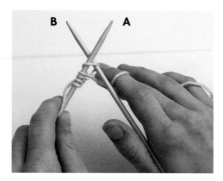

1 Insert a second needle (needle **B**) upward through the slipknot and behind the first needle (needle **A**).

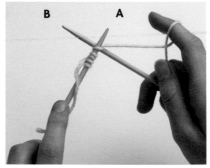

2 Take the long end of yarn from back to front around the tip of (needle **B**).

Cable cast-on

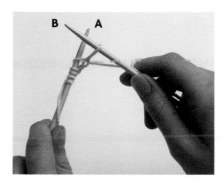

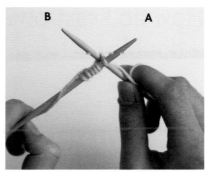

3 Bring (needle **B**), with its yarn, back down through the slipknot so making a new loop. Place this last loop onto (needle **A**). Repeat this procedure until you have enough stitches on (needle **A**), inserting (needle **B**) into the last loop made each time.

Work the first stages as before, but when you have two stitches (or loops) on needle **A**, insert needle **B** between them. Wrap the yarn around needle **B** as before and bring the needle back down between the stitches. Place the new loop on needle **A** and repeat this procedure, working between the stitches each time.

BELOW The left-hand side shows a knitted cast-on edge.

Question 21:
How do I cast on using a double cast-on?

This method, also known as the thumb method, only uses one needle; the other "needle" is your thumb! Make a slipknot as before, but this time several inches from the end of the yarn.

It will take approximately ¾ inches (2 cm) of yarn for each stitch so make sure that you measure out enough to complete your cast-on. If you run short you can either join in an extra length of yarn, which you will have to darn in at the end, or you can complete your cast-on using one of the two needle methods—but remember that this portion will look slightly different and may not be as elastic.

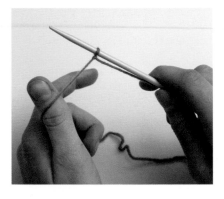

1 Place the slipknot on the needle. Hold the short end of yarn in the palm of your left hand and loop it over your thumb from back to front.

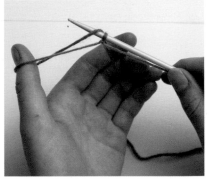

2 Insert the needle under the strand of yarn that runs from your thumb into your palm.

 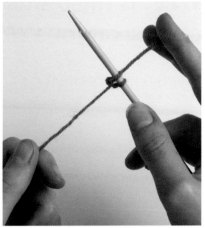

3 Wrap the long end of yarn around the needle from back to front and draw it through the loop around your thumb.

4 Pull on the short end of yarn to tighten the stitch on the needle. Repeat this until you have enough stitches.

Question 22:
Which method of casting on is the most hardwearing?

The cable cast-on is the strongest, but avoid knitting into the back of the stitches on the first row, as this can put unnecessary strain on them. Cable cast-on gives a firm edge with a definite ridge on the right side. To avoid this ridge work the first row as a purl row, remembering to make a note of this if you are following a pattern or counting rows.

Cable cast-on is even stronger if worked with one of the yarns doubled. This method is often used for Channel Island guernseys.

Question 23:
What is the best method of casting on for a ribbed hem?

If you don't want a noticeable edge to your cast-on when working a rib you will need to adopt one of the "invisible," or tubular, methods of casting on, such as this:

HOW IT'S DONE

Using a length of waste yarn in a contrast color and the loop method, cast on half the required number of stitches.
Row 1 Take up the main color and a second needle, and knit the first stitch. Bring the yarn forward between the needles, and then knit the second stitch. There will be an extra loop of yarn on the second needle between the stitches.

Repeat this to the end of the row.
Row 2 * Slip 1, with yarn at back knit the next stitch, repeat from * to end.
Row 3 As for Row 2, but beginning with the knit stitch.

Repeat these two rows once more and then work knit one, purl one rib or stockinette in the usual way, increasing one at the end of the row if you need an odd number of stitches. When the rib is complete, remove the contrast yarn.

BELOW The waste yarn can be seen at bottom left of the sample.

Question 24:
Which method of casting on gives the most elastic edge?

The double cast-on is the most elastic. For this reason it is especially useful for hats, socks, and gloves where the piece must be able to stretch sufficiently to go over a wider part of the body and then shrink back to grip firmly.

The double cast-on has another advantage in that it can be worked in two different yarns or colors at the same time without losing its elasticity, creating a decorative edge.

Alternatively a length of very fine, almost transparent elastic can be held together with the yarn and knitted in with it at the same time. But beware of using this elastic with white yarn, especially cotton, as it can change the color, giving it a grubby appearance.

Question 25:
Is there a way of estimating the length of "tail" yarn needed for casting on by the double cast-on?

The most basic guide is to leave a length of yarn at least three times the width of the finished piece of work. It is best to err on the generous side, because a long tail can be used for stitching the seam later.

If you run out before you have enough stitches, add a few more using one of the two-needle methods. But remember that the different cast-ons all have a slightly different appearance. Knitted cast-on is a loose edge, useful for picking up stitches for hems, and so on, loop cast-on leaves a very soft edge, and double cast-on leaves a ridge on the right side. This can be avoided if the first row is worked as a purl row; don't forget to adjust your row counts to accommodate this.

Question 26:
What is the best method of casting on for lace knitting?

If you want to produce a soft edge to the lace—one that is not going to be joined to another edge—the loop cast-on will be ideal, especially if it is worked with needles one size larger than those for the main work. It will have no hard edge but will leave a row of small loops compatible with an open, lacy pattern.

Place a slipknot on the right-hand needle. * Wrap yarn from back to front around the left thumb. Catch the strand nearest to the palm with the point of the needle from back to front and pull it taught. Repeat from *.

For an edge that is to be joined to another, or picked up and knitted in the opposite direction, use a provisional cast-on.

Take a long length of waste yarn about four times the width of the finished knitting and hold it alongside a needle one or two sizes larger than the size being used for the main work. Fasten the main yarn to the same needle with a slipknot. Holding the yarns taut with the left hand, * take the main yarn under the waste yarn then up behind it and over the needle from front to back. Bring the main yarn down again to pass in front of the waste yarn (the movement of the needle describes a figure eight). Repeat from * for the required number of stitches. Knit the first row in the usual way, being careful not to catch the waste yarn, which will be drawn out after the work is finished to leave a row of loops.

LEFT Loop cast-on.

Question 27:
How many other ways are there to cast on?

There are several variations on the methods described above. The simplest changes are to twist the stitch before placing it on the needle, or to cast on purlwise. Some of these alterations make very little difference to the finished appearance, but you may prefer to work them in a different way. The loop cast-on can be twisted twice before being placed on the needle. It is less likely to slip off the needles than the basic loop cast-on, and it is easier to knit the first row.

The double cast-on can also be worked in different ways by holding the yarn over the left index finger or holding both strands of yarn in the left palm and using the needle to catch one strand and draw it through the other.

A method that was unique to Channel Island guernseys is the knotted cast-on, also based on the double cast-on.

Cast on two stitches; pass the first of them over the second. Repeat until you have the required number of stitches.

It will leave a row of small knots at the edge and is a strong, hard-wearing cast-on.

BELOW Knotted or Channel Island cast-on.

Question 28:
What is a picot edge?

Picots are small points or decorative knots, which are often used for baby garments or for decorating neck and cuff edges. They can be worked vertically or horizontally, but different methods are employed for each type of picot edge.

A vertical picot edge with prominent points is worked by casting on two or three stitches at the beginning of a row and then binding them off again before working the next stitches. A picot edge can also be made as a separate edging as in looped cast-on, to be sewn or knitted onto the main piece, or a row of small loops can be made at the beginning of the row by bringing the yarn forward before knitting two stitches together.

A horizontal edge can be worked by casting on and binding off stitches.

At the cast-on edge
* Cast on five, bind off two. Return the last stitch to the left-hand needle and repeat from * until you have the required number of stitches.

At the bound-off edge
Bind off three. * Draw a loop through the last stitch on the right-hand needle three or four times to make a short length of chain. Knit next stitch on left-hand needle and pass last chain over this stitch. Bind off one or two stitches and repeat from *.

Alternatively you could make a picot hem (see page 39).

EXPERT TIP

66 Use a crochet hook for a quicker way of making picots. Insert the hook under the first edge stitch, bring the yarn over the hook from back to front and draw it through both stitches on the hook; this makes one single crochet. Work thus along the edge to the end then turn the work and *make three chain; insert the hook back into the stitch at the bottom, yarn over and draw through. Work one or two single crochet then repeat from * to the end. 99

BELOW Picot edge.

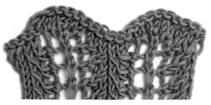

Question 29:
How do I make a picot hem?

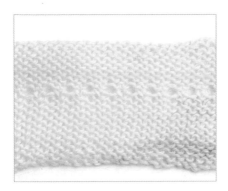

1 Using needles two sizes smaller than for the main body, cast on an odd number of stitches using the knit cast-on. Work a few rows in stockinette, ending with a purl row. Change to needles one size larger and make a row of eyelets as follows: * Knit one, bring yarn forward and knit the next two stitches together. Repeat from * to the end of the row.

2 Continue working in stockinette for the same length as before the eyelet row, beginning and ending with a purl row. Next row: fold the hem back with wrong sides on the inside and knit together one stitch from the needle with one from the cast-on row, to the end.

A picot hem can also be made at the finishing edge of a garment but the hem will then need to be stitched down.

Question 30:
Why is it sometimes difficult to knit into the cast-on row?

When you cast on, each time you place a new loop on the needle you draw up the yarn ready for the next one. You may be pulling this too tightly before beginning the next stitch. It might help to use a needle one or two sizes larger than that specified for the initial row. As you become more accustomed to casting on you will build up a natural rhythm that will help to keep an even tension on the yarn, making it easier to work.

If you have used the simple loop cast-on, take care not to let the loops slip off the needle before you have knitted them; it is very difficult to replace a dropped loop onto the needle once you have lost it. Loop cast-on is not a good method to use with slippery yarns such as silk or rayon.

Question 31:
How do I cast on when making a multicolored item?

Usually, unless a pattern states otherwise, you should cast on in your main color, but if you want to incorporate one of your contrast colors, try the double cast-on using two different colors. For a hardwearing edge, using whichever method you prefer, hold two different colors together for the cast-on row.

If you want a seamless transition into a color from your cast-on row then you will need to cast on with the colors according to the first row of your chart, choosing whichever method you wish and darning in your ends later. Remember that this could result in some strain on the stitches at the changeover points.

Multicolored ribs on Fair Isle garments are usually worked with the main color only for the cast-on row and the first row.

Question 32:
How do I make a looped edge?

Looped cast-on is a decorative edge in its own right and looks very pretty on babies' garments. It can also be useful for attaching a fringe. It is worked lengthwise with one edge of loops picked up and knitted to form the first row. Do not confuse it with loop or single cast-on, which is usually used for buttonholes or to give a soft edge to lace knitting.

Make a slipknot and cast on one stitch using the simple cast-on. Bring yarn forward, slip the next stitch purlwise, and knit the second stitch. Lift the slipped stitch over the knitted stitch. Turn and repeat this action until you have as many loops as required.

BELOW **A looped edge is a simple way to make a decorative edge on a plain garment.**

BASIC STITCHES

3

There are only two stitches used in knitting, knit and purl. But the different ways they are combined create an enormous variety of textures and shapes.

Question 33:
How do I make a knit stitch?

The knit stitch and its counterpart, the purl stitch, are the two basic stitches that make up all stitch patterns in knitting. The knit stitch forms an inverted "V" on the side that is facing you and a ridge on the reverse. The purl stitch forms a ridge on the side facing you and an inverted "V" on the reverse. These differences are used to create numerous stitch patterns.

1 After you have cast on a number of stitches, keep the yarn at the back of the work and insert the right-hand needle into the first stitch on the left-hand needle from front to back.

EXPERT TIP

66 Do not pull the yarn too tight as you make your stitches; they should glide easily along the needle so they are easy to work into on the next row. If you find that they are becoming too tight, try holding your yarn in a different way. **99**

2 Take the yarn around the back of the right-hand needle, and bring it forward between the two needle tips.

3 Gently withdraw the right needle tip, catching the loop of yarn that you have just made, and bring it through to rest on the needle, slipping the original stitch off the left needle at the same time. Do the same for each stitch until you reach the end of the row. Turn the work and change the needles over so that the knitted stitches are on the left, then knit the next row. Continue in this way for a few rows until you develop a rhythm and your knitting becomes smooth and even.

Here we show the first two stages of making a knit stitch with the yarn held in the left hand, this time using the Continental method.

Picture 2 shows the new loop drawn through the needle before the original stitch is slipped off.

Question 34:
How do I make a purl stitch?

1 As before, cast on a number of stitches. This time, however, keep the yarn in front of the needles.

2 Insert the right-hand needle into the front of the first stitch on the left needle from the back to the front. Take the yarn over the right needle, around the back, and bring it forward underneath the needle tip.

3 Gently push the tip of the right needle away from you, catching the loop of yarn with it, and slip the original stitch off the left needle. Repeat these movements to the end of the row, then turn the work so that the needles change hands, and begin the second row. Continue in this way for a few rows and you will notice that the piece looks just the same as your first sample, but probably not as firm and even! Don't worry, this is quite normal. Purl stitches are often more uneven than knit ones.

The same three stages for making a purl stitch as shown on the left, but this time holding the yarn in the left hand, using the Continental method.

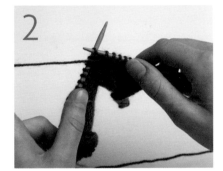

EXPERT TIP

66 Purl stitches are more awkward to work using the Continental method. If you prefer to hold the yarn in your left hand, either try tensioning it with your thumb instead of your index finger, or work in the round, when every row will then be knit. 99

Question 35:
What is garter stitch?

The two samples you have just made are known as garter stitch or "knit every row." The fabric is the same on both sides, and it lies flat when taken off the needles. These are the methods of working when using two needles and knitting back and forth, but to produce garter stitch when working in the round, alternate rows must be purled.

Garter stitch will stretch widthwise, and for this reason it was used to knit garters or stocking tops, while stockinette, which stretches lengthwise, was used for the stocking legs. It is a useful stitch for knitting items sideways, especially if you want to produce vertical stripes. It does not need an edging as it lies flat and does not curl, so it is often used at the edges of stockinette pieces or as borders to any other kind of stitch that has a tendency to roll up.

The number of rows in garter stitch is almost equal to the number of stitches, which makes it useful when working various triangular and diamond shapes. However, it has a tendency to stretch lengthwise during wear.

Question 36:
How do I work stockinette?

Stockinette, stocking stitch, or smooth knitting is produced when rows are worked alternately as knit and purl, unless you are knitting in the round, in which case every row is knit. The smooth side is usually the right side, but occasionally the other side of the fabric is used as the right side and then it is known as reverse stockinette.

When taken off the needles, stockinette fabric will curl inward to the wrong side at the sides, and out to the right side at the top and bottom. To prevent this, it is usually edged with a stitch that will lie flat. This can be garter stitch, but more often it is a rib or moss stitch at the bottom edge and, if the work is not being joined, garter or moss stitch at the sides.

The number of stitches to the inch is less than the number of rows in stockinette, but the exact ratio will depend on the yarn and the needle size. As a rough guide, knitting worsted on size 6 needles will give approximately five stitches and seven rows to the inch; on size 4 needles it will give six stitches and eight rows to the inch.

Question 37:
How do I count the rows in garter stitch?

In garter stitch the ridges appear alternately on the right and wrong sides of the fabric. So, count the number of ridges on one side and then double that number to get the number of rows you have worked. If you have a "smooth" row facing you on the right side of the work, you must add this row to your total to give the correct number. After you have cast on, the first row on the right side will appear as a smooth row, and the second row will be a "ridge" row. If you have just ended after a wrong side row, you will have a row of ridges on the right side and you will have worked an even number of rows.

Question 38:
How do I count the rows in stockinette stitch?

The simplest way to count the rows in flat knitting is to count the ridges on the reverse. Each ridge is one row.

If you are working in the round and have to count on the right side, then lay a rigid ruler alongside one column of stitches several rows down from the needles and count the number of "V"s. It can be very easy to miscount if you don't use a ruler as a marker, because your eye will have a tendency to travel across the rows.

EXPERT TIP

66 If you haven't been counting your rows as you go or you find it difficult to count them because of the type of yarn, for example, as long as you know your row gauge you can work out how many rows you have done by measuring your work. 99

RIGHT Chunky scarf worked in garter stitch.

Question 39:
How do I work into the back of a stitch?

Knitting into the backs of all the stitches causes them to appear twisted on the right side. It is more elastic than the stitch produced by working in the usual way.

To knit into the back of a stitch, insert the right-hand needle into the back loop of the stitch—in other words, behind the left-hand needle, instead of into the front—then work the stitch in the usual way. The new stitch will be twisted. If you want every stitch to appear twisted, then the purl stitches will also need to be worked into the backs.

Working a purl stitch is slightly more awkward, as the right-hand needle has to be turned away from you in order to come into the back of the purl stitch from left to right. When you have caught the stitch, bring the right-hand needle to the front of the left needle and finish the stitch in the normal way.

Knitting into the backs of stitches is most often used for twisted rib or for decreasing, but it can also be useful when you want to tighten up a stitch.

ABOVE Knitting into the back of a stitch.

ABOVE Purling into the back of a stitch.

ABOVE The top section has been worked into the back of the stitches on the knit rows only. The bottom section has been worked into the back of the stitches on the knit and purl rows.

Question 40:
How do I make a slip stitch?

A slip stitch is made by simply transferring it from the left needle to the right needle without working it. If you are working a knit row, slip it as though you were going to purl it, otherwise it will become twisted. Make sure that the yarn stays to the back on the knit rows unless the pattern instructs otherwise, or a short strand of yarn will be left across the front of the work. Don't pull the yarn tight before working the next stitch, but continue to maintain the same tension throughout.

If you are slipping the stitch in order to make a decrease, it should usually be slipped knitwise. Slip stitches on the purl rows should also be slipped purlwise, but this time, keep the yarn to the front unless the pattern instructs otherwise.

Question 41:
What is "ribbing"?

Ribbing, or rib, is a technique used to draw in the knitted fabric. It is a two-row pattern made by alternating numbers of knit and purl stitches on the first row and then on the following row, purling the stitches that were knitted previously, and vice versa. There are also various "broken ribs," where alternate rows are knitted or purled. These broken ribs are usually worked as a main pattern since they are not as elastic as standard rib. The number of knit stitches and purl stitches usually match, as this gives the most elastic rib; the more stitches that are worked in one stitch before changing to the other, the less elastic the piece will be. If the ribbing is used for hems, cuffs, collars, and so on, it is usually worked on needles two sizes smaller than those for the main part; the smaller the needles, the more it will draw in.

Ribbing is also frequently used for scarves as it does not curl and it is reversible. Columns of ribbed stitches can also be combined with cables to form an attractive hem, often seen in Aran garments.

Question 42:
What are 1 x 1 or 2 x 2 rib?

As described on page 53, true ribbing is made by alternating knit and purl stitches.

To work 1 x 1 rib

Cast on an odd number of stitches; knit one, purl one, alternately ending with a knit stitch. On the following row purl those stitches that were knitted, which will now look like purl stitches on the wrong side, and knit those stitches that were purled and now look like knit stitches. Continue knitting one stitch and purling one alternately.

If knitting in the round, work over an even number of stitches and knit one, purl one alternately to the end.

To work 2 x 2 rib

Knit two, purl two alternately over a number of stitches divisible by four. Follow the pattern as set for each row. If you have ended with purl two, the next row will begin with knit two.

The number of knit and purl stitches can be as varied as you wish but the more stitches of each kind there are, the less elastic the piece will be.

Question 43:
How do I work into the row below?

To work "knit one below" or "purl one below" as part of a pattern, insert the tip of the needle into the stitch directly below the next one on the left-hand needle, work it in the usual way, and slip both "old" stitches of the needle together.

This technique cannot be used over adjacent stitches or the row below will begin to unravel. At least the following stitch must be worked in the normal way. Stitches can also be made from those several rows below, but they are usually pulled into a long loop before being placed on the needle.

A form of knit or purl one below is also used to make an increase, but this time a new stitch is made from the stitch below and then the original stitch is also worked before both stitches are placed on the right-hand needle.

Question 44:
Which is the best rib to use at the hem of a sweater?

The rib that draws in the most is 2 x 2 rib. If you do not want your hem to be quite as clingy, use one of the other combinations or purl all the wrong side rows. Do not simply use larger needles, because the rib will eventually become loose and baggy.

All of the above information about ribs must be modified if you are knitting with silk or cotton, as these fibers don't have much elasticity of their own. They will look fine when you are working them, but they will soon lose their shape with wear. This can be remedied to some extent by knitting-in elastic, but it is probably better to choose some other type of edging for these materials and not to knit the kind of garment that requires a fitted hem.

Question 45:
What is twisted rib?

Twisted rib is a variation on 1 x 1 rib. It is worked by knitting into the back of the knit stitches on the right side rows and purling into the back of them on the wrong side rows. It gives a much firmer rib and makes the knit stitches stand out more. The knit stitches are simple to work, since the movements are the same as for standard rib except that the right-hand needle is inserted into the back of the stitch. Purl stitches are a little more awkward to work, as the right-hand needle has to be twisted back through the stitch first. For this reason, twisted rib is often worked on the right sides only, with just the knit stitches being twisted and the purl stitches worked as normal. On the wrong side, both stitches are worked in the normal way.

As well as being used at the edges of garments, twisted rib is often used as a divider between columns of Aran patterns.

Question 46:
What is fisherman's rib?

Fisherman's rib is another variation on 1 x 1 rib, but one that produces a softer feel to the fabric. An example of fisherman's rib is shown right.

Fisherman's rib is another reversible fabric—useful for scarves—and looks best worked on slightly larger needles than you would normally use.

HOW IT'S DONE

Cast on an odd number of stitches and knit the first row. Now repeat the following two rows.

Row 1 Slip 1, * knit 1 below, purl 1, repeat from * to end.

Row 2 Slip 1, * purl 1, knit 1 below, repeat from * to last 2 stitches, purl 1, knit 1.

Always slip the first stitch of the row for a firm edge.

A similar pattern can be produced by working every row after the foundation row thus:

Bring yarn forward, slip one purlwise, knit two together.

This version is usually known as brioche rib.

Question 47:
What is half fisherman's rib?

This is similar to fisherman's rib, but is not the same on both sides—although both sides are attractive and it is your choice as to which one you use as the right side.

Work the foundation row and Row 1 as for fisherman's rib, but work alternate rows as all knit or as 1 x 1 rib without knitting into the row below.

Fisherman's rib, brioche rib, and half fisherman's rib all produce soft, double-thickness fabrics that are warm without feeling bulky. They are ideal for Afghans and blankets, especially when worked with very large needles, as the gap between

the two layers traps air. However, because it takes two rows of knitting to produce one row of stitches they have more rows to the inch than usual and take longer to work.

Question 48:
How do I make long stitches?

Making a row of long stitches every so often will make the work grow quickly.

They are not really suitable for garments as they are too open, but they make attractive scarves and stoles and are a quick way of working long straight pieces for Afghans, especially with thicker yarn.

EXPERT TIP

66 Another way of making long stitches is to use a needle several sizes larger for some rows. This is an ideal way of making long rows where you are working a more complicated pattern stitch. 99

1 Long stitches are made by wrapping the yarn more than once, usually three times, around the right-hand needle before knitting the stitch, then dropping the extra loops on the following row.

2 The basic version is to wrap the yarn on every stitch of every right side row, and knit the following wrong side rows. But any number of plain rows, or rows in another stitch pattern, can be worked in between the long stitch row.

3 Long stitches can also be knitted together on the return row to give a lacy look. Increases must be made on the following row to compensate for the decreases. Alternatively, they can be worked in groups placed between a few knit stitches to give a waved effect, or they can be interlaced.

Question 49:
How do I make interlaced stitches?

You will need a multiple of eight stitches, as follows:

Work the first row for long stitch by wrapping the yarn around the needle as shown on the previous page. Then on the following row:

Slip one, dropping the extra wraps, eight times (eight long stitches on the right needle). With the point of the left needle lift the first four loops (those furthest away from the point of the right-hand needle) over the second four (being careful not to twist them) and hold them on the left-hand needle. Transfer the remaining four loops to the left-hand needle and then knit them in that order. Repeat from * for each group of eight.

Work a few plain rows or a pattern of your choice between each set of interlacing as above.

Question 50:
How do I make butterfly stitch?

Butterfly stitch is made by slipping an odd number of stitches, say five, on alternate rows and then lifting and knitting together these strands on a later row.

This looks attractive as an all-over pattern with the butterflies alternated. Like most stranded patterns, because there are less loops in some rows, it is not very elastic.

BELOW Completed butterfly stitch is shown below, with the first stages shown right.

HOW IT'S DONE

Cast on a number of stitches divisible by ten, plus five.
Row 1 * Knit 5, bring yarn to front, slip next 5, take yarn to back, repeat from * to end, knit 5.
Row 2 and every alternate row Purl to end.
Rows 3, 5, 7, and 9 As Row 1.
Row 11 * Knit 7, lift the long strands and knit them together with the next stitch, knit 2, repeat from * to end.

Question 51:
How do I make knitted pleats?

A pleated effect can be made by combining narrow and wide rib, for example, seven stitches of 1 x 1 rib followed by six stitches of knit three, purl three. The wider band of knit stitches will fold over the purl ones to give a pleated appearance.

True pleats are made by working in either stockinette or a wide rib, but slipping the edge stitches where each fold line will be.

At the top of each pleat the folds are accordianed at the slipped stitches by knitting two stitches together.

ABOVE Pleats closed.
BELOW Pleats open.

HOW IT'S DONE

Cast on a number of stitches divisible by 13.
Row 1 * (Knit 2, slip 1 purlwise, purl 1), repeat portion in brackets once more, knit 2, slip 1 purlwise, purl 2, repeat from * to the end.
Row 2 Knit 2 (purl 3, knit 1) twice, purl 3, repeat from * to the end.
Repeat these two rows.

Question 52:
What is brocade knitting?

Brocade patterns are made by working purl stitches on the right side of a stockinette background. They can be extremely intricate and based on natural objects or geometric designs, such as those found in guernsey patterns.

A combination of knit and purl stitches traps more air, helping the wearer to retain more warmth. That is why many guernsey patterns have designs over the chest, yoke, and upper portion of the sleeves.

The designs are worked from charts and are very attractive while being simple to work. The sample is copied from the design on the silk shirt that King Charles I was said to have worn on the day of his execution.

Question 53:
What are "traveling stitches"?

Traveling stitches are those that change direction. They can be single stitches or multiples, and they can form various patterns, including cables, lattice, and honeycombs. They produce a raised texture and are most familiar to us through Aran patterns.

Single traveling stitches are made by working the second stitch on the needle before the first one. The different ways of doing this will be explained later.

Where multiple stitches need to be made to move across the fabric, another needle, known as a cable needle, is employed. The stitches to be moved are held on the cable needle while the others are worked, then those from the cable needle are transferred to the left-hand needle and worked as instructed.

If the stitches are moved in the same direction on every row it gives the appearance of a raised band traveling diagonally across the background. If the direction of travel is alternated, the stitches look like a vertical band of rope. Varying the direction of travel can produce all kinds of shapes, all of which will give a double thickness of fabric at the point where the stitches cross. For this reason, traveling stitches are often used for outdoor garments.

Question 54:
What is a "welt" and how do I make one?

Welts are the opposite of ribs; they extend the fabric widthwise, and are made by alternately knitting two or more rows then purling one or more rows. The purl rows will look more prominent than the knit rows, unlike purl stitches in ribbing, which seem to disappear into the fabric.

The photograph shows a version of "Wager Welt," so called because the onlooker was supposed to guess how many purl rows were in the pattern.

Welts can also be used in combination with matching rib patterns to give a basket weave effect. The simplest of these is to work knit two, purl two rib for two rows, then work one knit row followed by one purl row. There are any number of variations on this theme, some of which look quite complicated to do but are actually only groups of rib stitches alternated with the same number of rows of welting.

Even more complex basket weave patterns can be made by mixing ribs and welts on the same row for several rows, then reversing their positions for the next few rows.

TO MAKE A WELT

Row 1 Knit.
Row 2 Purl.
Row 3-8 Knit.

TO PRODUCE A BASKET WEAVE

Cast on a number of stitches divisible by six.
Row 1 Knit 3, purl 3.
Row 2 Knit 3, purl 3.
Row 3 Knit.
Row 4 Purl.
Row 5 Knit.
Row 6 Knit 3, purl 3.
Row 7 Knit 3, purl 3.
Row 8 Knit 3, purl 3.
Row 9 Knit.
Row 10 Knit.
Row 11 Purl.

Question 55:
How do I stop the edges curling back on a scarf?

If you are using a stitch that has a natural tendency to curl, such as stockinette or one of its lacy variations, you will need to plan ahead and either add extra stitches at each side or choose a different stitch for some of the side stitches and remember to account for these if working a pattern stitch. Work two or three stitches in garter stitch, moss stitch, or rib at the beginning and end of every row.

Some fabrics, especially lacy ones, will straighten out if they are pressed under a very damp cloth, but don't do this if you have a lot of textured pattern as you will flatten it. And don't use a hot iron and a lot of pressure with synthetic yarns, as they will end up flat and wide.

BELOW A few stitches worked in garter stitch will stop the edges from curling.

Question 56:
What edge stitch should I use for lace knitting?

If the edges are not being joined and the pattern doesn't specify, a very decorative edge is formed by bringing the yarn forward at the beginning of every row and then knitting two stitches together. This gives a row of small single-strand loops. Working the yarn forward without the decrease at the beginning of each row will create an outward sloping edge that will form a triangular shape. To reverse the slope and give a diamond shape, work a double decrease, in other words, knit three together after the yarn forward at the beginning of each row. This technique is often used to form the center of a Shetland shawl. The loops that are made are then used to pick up the stitches for the border.

If the edges of the lace are to be joined, use a garter stitch or slip stitch chain edging and a flat seam for sewing them together. Place right sides together and oversew as close to the edge as possible.

If you can crochet, an alternative method of joining lace is to crochet the seam together. Using the same yarn and a fine crochet hook, work a single crochet into the first loop on the side seam, then make one chain and a single crochet into the first loop on the other seam. Continue to work back and forth through each loop, making one chain in between.

EXPERT TIP

❝ For a more decorative edge to a shawl or scarf, consider making a narrow border long enough to go all around it. You can either sew it on at the end, or pick up some stitches from the straight edges of the border and attach the rest as you go by, knitting them together with the last stitch of the main section. Stitch down the remaining portion at the end. ❞

Question 57:
What is "moss stitch"?

Moss stitch, sometimes known as seed stitch, is a combination of knit and purl stitches, worked alternately as in rib, but then the placement of the stitches is staggered on the following row so that purl stitches are placed above knit stitches.

ABOVE Irish moss stitch (top of sample); moss stitch (bottom of sample).

TO MAKE MOSS STITCH

Cast on an odd number of stitches.
* **Row 1 and all rows** Knit 1, purl 1.

In Britain and Europe this version is known as moss stitch. It is a slightly wider stitch than stockinette, but not as wide as garter stitch. It will lie flat and won't curl, so it is useful for edgings. However, there are several variations of moss stitch, and some patterns may describe it as being worked over four rows instead of two.

Cast on an even number of stitches.
* **Row 1 and 2** Knit 1, purl 1.
* **Row 3 and 4** Purl 1, knit 1.

This version is sometimes known as Irish moss stitch.

There is also a version worked over four stitches and four rows. It is variously known as Irish moss stitch (again), double moss stitch, or box stitch.

TO MAKE THIS VERSION

Cast on a number of stitches divisible by four.
Row 1 and 2 Knit 2, purl 2.
Row 3 and 4 Purl 2, knit 2.

Unlike moss stitch these two patterns will not have a widthwise stretch and will have a similar tension to stockinette. This is why they are often used in combination with Aran stitches and possibly why they became known as Irish moss stitch.

Question 58:
Which is the best edge stitch for joining pieces together?

This depends to a large extent on which method you prefer to use for sewing. The neatest seam is made using mattress stitch, and this is easiest to do if you knit the first and last stitch of every row, although it is equally invisible if you have worked the whole row in the pattern stitch.

Work with right sides facing you, side by side, and take the sewing needle under the first stitch, or one stitch in from the edge, from each side alternately.

If you are going to backstitch seams, or need an edge from which to pick up stitches later, use a slip stitch edging, which is made by slipping the first stitch of every row. This edge is also useful for lace as it helps to keep the seam as loose as the rest of the knitting.

Where you need to join ribbed edges together, plan to begin and end the rib with the number of stitches that will look as close as possible to the rest of the ribbing when the seams are joined.

Question 59:
Why are my edge stitches loose?

You may be holding your stitches too far from the tip of the needle, or leaving too much slack in the yarn as you turn your work. Try pulling the yarn a little tighter on the first stitch, or working a purl stitch at the beginning of the knit rows and a knit stitch at the beginning of the purl rows.

It is also possible that it is your method of holding the yarn that is causing the loose stitch. Try different methods of working, and as you become more relaxed and comfortable with your knitting you will find that your stitches will even out.

If the pieces are to be joined together, the loose edge stitches will not matter too much if you sew the seams together with a backstitch one full stitch in from the edge.

BINDING OFF

4

Binding off is the technique used at the end of a piece of work to stop the stitches from unraveling. It needs to be as firm, but it should also be as flexible as the knitting itself.

Question 60:
How do I bind off?

As with casting on, there is more than one method of binding off, but the most basic is worked as shown by the three steps below.

If you are binding off on a purl row, don't use knit stitches or you will be left with a row of ridges that will look out of place on the right side. This is less important if these edges are to be seamed or have stitches picked up from them. Bind off with purl stitches, lifting the stitch from the back if you find that the strand of yarn gets in your way.

1 Knit the first two stitches, then lift the first one over the second one; there is now one stitch on the right-hand needle.

2 Knit the next stitch and lift the stitch from the right-hand needle over it. Continue like this to the end of the row, leaving one stitch on the right-hand needle each time.

3 Break off the yarn and pass it through the last stitch on the needle. Draw it up firmly and fasten off.

Question 61:
Why is my bind-off row tight?

You may be knitting the stitches too tightly or pulling too firmly on the stitch as you lift it over its neighbor. It may help to use a needle one or two sizes larger for the bind-off row.

Alternatively, try working with a crochet hook. Again, choose one that is a size larger and hold it as you would hold your right-hand needle. Work the first two stitches then pull the second one through the first, drawing up the loop as large as you like.

A different method of binding off that helps to prevent tightening is to leave two stitches on the right-hand needle before working the third. The first two stitches are bound off as usual, but the stitch is kept on the left needle while the third stitch is knitted by bringing the right needle in front of the left and into the third stitch from left to right. Both stitches are then slipped off the left needle, making two on the right one. The first of these is passed over the second, and the process is repeated until all the stitches have been bound off. This edge will not be as firm as the usual bind-off, but nor will it ever be tight.

Question 62:
Should I bind off in colors if I am following a color chart?

If you are joining shoulder seams by the invisible seaming method, or if you are attaching a set-in sleeve, there will be a less noticeable seam if you continue with the same colors as on the last row of the chart. Use the correct colors for sewing up, too, especially if some of them are a strong contrast.

Try to finish a chart on a row that does not have part of a large motif at that point; or better still, finish on a row worked in one color. If you are to pick up stitches from a row with several blocks of color, it will blend in better if you use the same color for your bind-off row as is used to pick up and knit the first row of stitches.

Question 63:
Should I bind off in the same stitch as the pattern?

Most knitting instructions tell you this, but assuming they do not, you can make a neater edge if you continue to follow any combination of knit and purl stitches when you bind off. If you are working cables, do not bind off on a cable row but finish halfway between crossovers; then, when you join shoulder seams, there will be an equal number of rows between all the cables.

If you are joining moss stitch with a three-needle bind-off, finish with the same stitches facing each other and bind off with their opposite stitch.

If you are knitting a scarf or any other piece where both edges may be seen at the same time, try to match the cast-on edge to the bound-off edge. For a lacy pattern try making a knitted edging, working the last stitch of this with one of the stitches from the edge of the main piece and, at the cast-on edge, either knitting it on or stitching it to the cast-on row. Alternatively, if you plan ahead you can make this edging first and then pick up the stitches from it for the rest of the scarf.

BELOW The right-hand top edge of the sample is bound off in pattern, and the left-hand top edge is bound off with knit stitches.

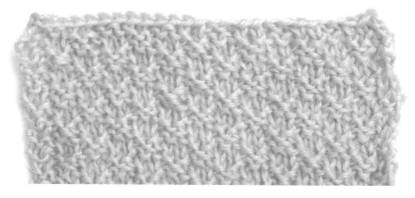

RIGHT Bound-off edge of scarf follows the pattern of stripes.

Question 64:
What is a "three-needle bind-off"?

A three-needle bind-off is often used for joining shoulder edges, or for joining the toes of socks that have been knitted from the top down.

1 Work the last row before binding off, then place both shoulders together with right sides facing and with needle tips pointing the same way.

2 With a third needle, knit through the first stitch on the front shoulder and the first stitch on the back shoulder.

3 Leave the new stitch made on the right-hand needle. Do the same with both of the next stitches, then pass the first stitch made over the second stitch. Repeat this action to the end of the row.

4 Maintain the stitch color or pattern on the bind-off row as described on page 74.

Question 65:
How do I work a picot edge bind-off?

There are at least two methods of knitting a picot edge at the end of a piece of knitting. The first one makes quite prominent picots.

Bind off one stitch, * insert the right-hand needle into the next stitch and cast on two or three stitches, bind off four, then slip the last stitch back onto the left-hand needle and repeat from * to end.

You can make the picots as large as you like by casting on more stitches, but remember to bind off one more than you have cast on each time.

The second method leaves a row of small loops.

Bind off three stitches in the usual way, * draw a loop through the stitch on the right-hand needle three times (in other words, make three chains), knit the next stitch, pass the last chain stitch over the knit stitch, bind off one (or however many you want between picots), then repeat from * to end.

A third method for those who can crochet is to work the picots with a crochet hook.

Use the same size hook as the needles with which you were knitting. * Draw a loop of yarn through the first stitch on the needle, repeat for the second stitch, and draw this stitch through the first one. Make three chains and work a slip stitch, or a single crochet into the first of them. Repeat from *, working as many bound-off stitches as you wish between picots.

Question 66:
How do I avoid a loose stitch at the end of a bind-off row?

This loose stitch is almost inevitable, but it can be made slightly less noticeable if you work the last two stitches together, or work the last stitch into the row below.

If neither of these methods work, thread a blunt-ended needle with the tail end of yarn left after the last stitch. Take the needle down into the stitch of the row below and work over it as for duplicate stitch (see page 181). Duplicate stitch the loose stitch. If there is still a loose strand catch it down into the back of the work a row or two below.

Question 67:
When would I use a provisional bind-off?

A provisional bind-off is the simplest way to remove stitches from the needles without letting them unravel! Simply thread a blunt-ended needle with a long length of contrast yarn and pass it through all of the stitches left on the knitting needle. Tie the ends together firmly. If you use a fairly slippery yarn and one that is not thicker than the yarn you are knitting with, it will withdraw more easily.

A provisional bind-off can be used:

- If you are to stop knitting for a long period of time—leaving it on the needles will cause a distortion of the stitches.
- If you want to measure your knitting more accurately.
- If you want to attach a fringe to your knitting—attach the fringe through the open loops before removing the contrast yarn.
- If you need to graft two pieces together.
- If you want to gather the edge of your knitting.

Question 68:
How do I work an invisible bind-off?

Invisible bind-off is usually worked on single rib, but it can also be used on stockinette. It is made in a similar way to grafting with a sewing needle threaded with the long tail of yarn left at the end of the knitting. This tail end needs to be at least four times the width of your finished piece and at the right-hand end of the work with the right side facing you.

Assuming that your first stitch is a knit stitch:

Insert the sewing needle knitwise into the first stitch and take it off the knitting needle. Insert it purlwise into the next knit stitch on the knitting needle, then back into the purl stitch (the first one on the needle). Pull the yarn up gently and drop the first stitch off the knitting needle. Insert the sewing needle knitwise into the next purl stitch and pull the yarn through. Continue in this way, following the shape of the stitches, until they are all worked off.

SHAPING

Different shapes are achieved by using increases and decreases to make the knitting wider or narrower at various points. Increases and decreases can also be used to form various stitch patterns.

Question 69:
How do I work a decrease?

When a pattern says decrease at each end of the row it usually means knit (or purl) two stitches together. There are several ways of doing this, but the most common are

- Knit two together = insert the right needle from left to right through the next two stitches and knit them as one.
- Knit two together through back loop = as in twisted stitches.
- Slip one, knit one, pass slipped stitch over = slip the first stitch knitwise, knit the next stitch and pass the slipped stitch over the knitted one.
- Slip, slip, knit = slip the first stitch knitwise, then do the same with the second one, insert the left needle into these stitches from left to right and knit them together.

Similar movements are made for purling two stitches together but in the last method described here the two stitches are slipped purlwise and then put back, twisted, onto the left-hand needle before being purled together through the back.

BELOW Ways of working decreases as described in the text.

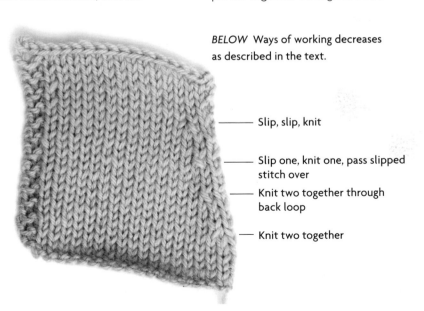

——— Slip, slip, knit

——— Slip one, knit one, pass slipped stitch over

— Knit two together through back loop

— Knit two together

Question 70:
How do I decrease several stitches together?

The usual requirement is for three stitches to be worked into one. Again, there are several methods of doing this, some of which are

• Knit three together = insert the right needle from left to right through all three stitches and knit them as one.
• Slip, slip, knit = slip the first stitch knitwise, then slip the second stitch knitwise, knit the next stitch, insert the left-hand needle through the two slipped stitches and pass them over the third stitch.
• Slip one, knit two together, pass slipped stitch over.

• Slip, hold, slip: slip the first stitch knitwise, hold the next stitch at the back of the work, slip the third stitch knitwise, place the held stitch onto the right-hand needle, insert the left-hand needle from left to right into the front of the three stitches and knit them as one.
• Hold the first stitch at the back, slip one, place the held stitch on the left needle and knit it together with the next stitch, pass the slipped stitch over.

BELOW **Ways of decreasing several stitches as described in the text.**

Hold, slip one, knit two together, pass slipped stitch over

Slip, hold, slip

Slip one, knit two together, pass slipped stitch over

Slip, slip, knit

Knit three together

Question 71:
Does it matter which of these methods I use to decrease?

You will see, if you work a decrease using the methods described on page 82, that there is an obvious directional slope, and the method you select will make a difference to the finished appearance of your work.

Knit two together slopes toward the right. Knit two together through back loop; slip one, knit one, pass slipped stitch over; and slip, slip, knit all slope toward the left, but this last technique is the best match for knit two together, as it does not distort the stitch underneath.

Not all patterns will give precise instructions about which method to use, but even if they do you may think that another method is more suitable. Sometimes, at a neck edge or in raglan shaping, you may want the decreases to slope in the same direction as the edge, especially so when you are decreasing at the extreme edge of the work and this stitch will be taken into the seam. If you want a more decorative effect you may want to slant them in the opposite direction to the seam and work them a few stitches in from the edge.

Question 72:
How do I increase a stitch?

There are several ways to increase within a row. The third of these is the neatest and is sometimes called "invisible increase." They can also be worked on purl stitches:

• Knit to where the increase is to be placed, then lift the small horizontal strand between the stitches onto the left needle and knit it. This will leave a small hole, but if you knit into the back of the stitch it will be less obtrusive (**A**).

• Knit the stitch as usual, but before slipping it off the needle knit again into the back of it (**B**).

- Lift the stitch directly below the next one to be worked and knit it, then knit the stitch on the needle (**C**).
- Knit to the point where the increase is to be made, bring yarn over then continue to the end of the row. On the next row, twist the yarn over by working into the back of it (**D**).

To add several stitches at the beginning of a row use one of the plainer methods of casting on. To add stitches in the middle of a row, either use the loop cast-on or one of the methods described on page 87.

BELOW Four different methods of increasing a stitch, as described in the text.

A

B

C

D

Question 73:
Which stitch should I use to make the increase?

Most patterns will give precise instructions as to which stitch should be used for the increase, especially at armhole and neck shapings. However, if the pattern simply instructs you to increase at each end of the row, this often means one stitch in from the edge. If you think this might spoil a stitch pattern or a multicolored design, use the edge stitch by knitting into it through the front and back.

Where increases are to be made at both ends of a row and form a smooth, uninterrupted line, work them the same distance in from the edge.

Work the edge stitch, then increase by lifting the strand before the next stitch and knitting into the back of it. Continue until there is one stitch left on the needle, then lift the strand before it and knit into the back of it. These increases will be one stitch in from the edge, but any number of stitches can be worked before and after the increase.

Invisible increases can be matched in the same way, by lifting and knitting the head of the stitch of the row below before the stitch on the needle at the beginning of the row and after knitting the stitch on the needle at the end.

EXPERT TIP

" In garter stitch an increase or decrease at the beginning of every row will give a regular slope of 45 degrees. This feature can be utilized to make exact squares or triangles of any size. "

Question 74:
How do I make several stitches out of one?

There are some stitch patterns that require you to increase several stitches at once, particularly bobbles and lace patterns.

The methods used most frequently are:

- Knit, purl, knit, purl, knit all into the same stitch.
- Knit, yarn forward, knit, yarn forward, knit all into the same stitch.
- Wrap yarn several times around needle, and then on the return row work alternately into the front and then the back, or work alternately knit and purl.
- Horizontal buttonholes also need extra stitches and these are usually cast on by the loop cast-on method, which is why it is often called buttonhole cast-on.

The finished products of the first two methods described here do not look very different, whichever method is used. After the increases, a few rows are worked on these extra stitches and then decreased back to one again. The third method is mainly used in Shetland lace patterns to make a larger hole as in the "Crown of Glory," or Cat's Paw.

ABOVE **Making stitches in accordance with the first method described left.**

ABOVE **A few rows worked on the extra stitches.**

Question 75:
What is "paired" shaping?

As you will have seen if you have worked samples of shaping, some stitches slope to the left and some to the right. These shapings have a smooth line when worked in pairs, slanting to the left at the beginning of a row and to the right at the end. This is often a feature of raglan shaping where several stitches are worked before and after the decreases. Usually these edge stitches will be continued in stockinette, but the seam looks attractive if garter or moss stitch or even narrow cables are used.

If you want to make paired decreases more prominent on a stockinette background, work a double decrease every fourth row instead of one on every alternate row. Either work three stitches together using one of the methods described on page 83, or work two matching decreases side by side. Work them a few stitches in from the edge so that they don't get lost in the seams, and slope them in the opposite direction to the edge.

RIGHT Shaping inside a cable.

Question 76:
What is "full-fashioned" shaping?

Full-fashioned shaping is usually used on armhole and sleeve edges, especially fitted or semifitted ones, where decreasing at the extreme edge would make an untidy seam and where the garment is not meant to be loose fitting but shaped to the body. The decreasing is meant to be visible and is sometimes the only decoration on an otherwise plain garment.

At one time it was considered a feature of more expensive knitted items, as it was time-consuming to produce on a knitting machine.

The decreases are worked as pairs, using whichever methods seem most appropriate, four or five stitches in from each side. They are sometimes worked in the opposite direction to the slope of the edge in order to make them even more prominent. The edge stitches are usually left plain, but if they are more elaborate then the decreases are more likely to follow the line of the slope.

RIGHT **Shaping worked in the opposite direction to the shape.**

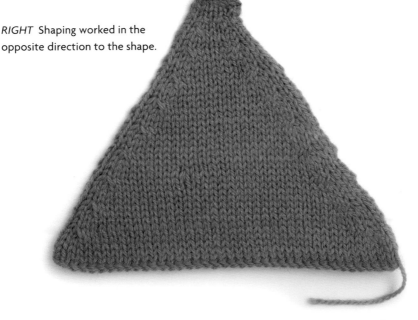

Question 77:
How do I purl two together through the back?

There are times when you need to decrease on the wrong side of a piece of work—for instance where shapings are worked regularly over an odd number of rows. Purling two together at the beginning of the row is straightforward, but purling two together at the end necessitates working them through the back in order to slope them the correct way—a slightly awkward operation, since the right needle must be turned through 180 degrees in order to enter the stitches from left to right. Loosen them a little with the tip of the right-hand needle, then insert the needle from left to right through the second stitch on the left-hand needle, then through the first, and purl them off as one.

An easier method, and one that mimics more closely the slip, slip, knit decrease, is to purl the next stitch and return it to the left-hand needle, lift the following stitch over it, then return the single stitch to the right needle.

Both methods will form a slant to the left on the right side of the work, but the second one is easier to work and has a neater finish.

Question 78:
How do I make mitered corners?

Mitered corners can be worked outward by working increases, or inward by working decreases. The former are sometimes used as edgings to cardigans or jackets where the stitches are picked up around the whole piece after it has been joined together. To make it work successfully the increasing must be done precisely at the corner of the piece.

To work a mitered corner from the edge outward, pick up the stated number of stitches around the edge, and mark the corner stitch with markers or contrast yarn. On the next row, increase at

ABOVE Working outward
with increases at corner.

ABOVE Working inward with
increases at corner.

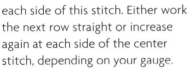

each side of this stitch. Either work
the next row straight or increase
again at each side of the center
stitch, depending on your gauge.

If you are making a right-angled
turn, a double increase on every
alternate row will usually work,
but it does depend on the stitch
used and you might need to alter
the frequency for stockinette. It
is best to work a test piece first.

If the edging is to be folded back
to form a hem, work decreases to
correspond with the increases made
in the first part, then fold the hem
back and stitch it down on the inside.

At V-necks, where the angle is
sharper, decreases are usually worked
on every row.

Either use one of the double
decrease methods where three
stitches are made into one, or work
paired decreases at each side of
the central stitch, which can be
either knit or purl, as you prefer.

An alternative method of working
a mitered corner is to leave two
stitches unworked at the end of each
alternate row until there are only two
left working, then take two back into
work again on each alternate row.

Question 79:
What does "work straight" mean?

This is a term used to denote that there will be no shaping of any kind on the next few rows, although any stitch pattern will be maintained. It is usually used to indicate the length of a particular piece, for example, the length from the top of the rib to the armhole shaping, or the length to the shoulders after the armhole shaping is finished.

Sometimes a pattern will give instructions to "work straight for x inches" and sometimes the instruction will be to "work x rows straight." If you have not obtained the correct row gauge, then following these instructions as they stand could cause problems later when it comes to shaping the sleeve head. The shaping on a sleeve head is calculated to fit a particular depth of armhole. If your row gauge is different you may need to calculate how many rows you must work here in order to be able to fit the sleeve in correctly. If you have fewer rows to the inch than the pattern states you will be working less rows at this point than the designer expects. When you come to shape the head of the sleeve, by the time you have completed the number of decreases stated in the pattern, your sleeve head will probably be much too big for the armhole. Either work the decreases more frequently or make your armhole longer.

LEFT Armhole edge worked straight after initial shaping.

Question 80:
How do I use shaping to make "zig-zags" or chevrons?

Chevron shapes and "zig-zags" are formed from bias fabrics, where the stitches appear to move diagonally across the piece instead of following each other vertically. Bias fabrics can slope either left or right depending on where the decreases and increases are made. If stitches are increased or decreased each side of one central stitch they will form chevrons, and the side edges will have a definite slope. If you increase in the center of a row and decrease at each end, the stitches will form a "V" shape but the sides will remain straight.

Stitches will fan out where they are increased, causing the line of stitches to point upward, and close in where they are decreased, causing it to point down. If a few rows of contrast color are introduced this will become more obvious.

Combining increasing with decreasing in the same row will produce zig-zag patterns. The piece illustrated was worked with a double decrease at the point of the "V"s, and an invisible increase at the beginning and end of the row and each side of the stitch at the top of the inverted "V"s.

BELOW This sample shows multicolored zig-zags or chevrons.

Question 81.
How do I know which stitches to increase in when the pattern says to "increase evenly across the row"?

This instruction is often given after the last row of rib. If there is no further information then you need to calculate the frequency of the increases for yourself. You don't need to be precise, but the garment hangs better if the increases are spaced more or less regularly. For example, if your last row had 74 stitches and you need to increase to 86, you know that you need 12 more stitches.

To space them evenly divide 74 by 11 (your first increase will come before the rest of the increases, so don't count it at this stage)—74 divided by 11 = six, remainder eight. Split the eight in half so that there are four at each end of the row, and then work the first increase after stitch four and the rest of them after every sixth stitch. If there is an odd number left after the division, work one extra stitch at the beginning or the end, it doesn't matter where.

To check that you have spaced your increases correctly, make a brief diagram with one mark for each stitch and a different mark for the increases.

Question 82:
How do I add darts to a sweater pattern?

Although knitted fabric is very flexible, there may be times when you want a more fitted shape. To make a fitted waist use decreases at the sides 3 or 4 inches (about 8–10 cm) in from the edge and starting a couple of inches up from the cast-on edge.

When you have reached the line of your waist, begin increasing at the same rate until you are back to the original number of stitches, or less if you have made the piece fuller at the beginning. Work the darts on the back and the front(s) of the piece.

If you find that some knitted garments ride up in front rather than sitting comfortably on the hips as intended, you may want to add darts at the bust. This will create more rows at the center, but the side edges of the front(s) should stay the same length as the back. Mark the stitch where you want the dart to end; a little below the center of the bust is usual. Work short rows, wrapping the yarn around the next stitch in the same way as for shaping shoulders, leaving about five stitches unworked on each row at the side edges. The actual number of unworked stitches depends on your gauge. When you have reached each of the marked stitches work across all the stitches, picking up the strands from the wraps and knitting them together with their stitch.

This method of working short row shaping is also used to create circular yokes, collars, and ruffles.

Question 83:
How do I shape shoulders without creating "steps"?

There are two ways of doing this depending on which method you are using to join the shoulders.

• If you are seaming the shoulders together bind off the first group of stitches then, on the return row, leave the last stitch on the needle and turn the work so that this is now the first stitch of the next row. Slip the first stitch on the left needle and pass the other stitch over it, then bind off the rest of the group of stitches.
• If you are grafting the stitches or using a three-needle bind-off, work back to the group of stitches to be bound off and leave them on the left-hand needle. Take the yarn to the other side of work and slip the next stitch purlwise onto the right-hand needle. Take the yarn to the original side and slip stitch back to the left needle. Turn and work back as far as the next group of stitches and repeat the process. When all the groups have been left, either work two rows across all stitches, picking up the strands and knitting them together with their related stitch, or join the shoulder seams and ignore the strands unless you are unhappy with their appearance.

6 IN THE ROUND

Knitting with circular or double-pointed needles makes it easier to follow charts. The technique also eliminates the need for sewing up afterward.

Question 84:
What are the advantages of working in the round?

Circular knitting, or knitting in the round, has several advantages.

• Its main advantage to most people is that there is little if any sewing up to be done after the work is finished.
• It is less tiring on the arms as the weight is evenly distributed, although the piece can get quite heavy as you near the end.
• The right side of the work is always facing you; this is ideal for working from charts because you can see the design as it looks on the page and you don't have to transcribe the charts in your head for the purl rows.
• If you leave knitting on a circular needle for any length of time, the stitches will not distort if they are all resting on the cord at the center.
• You can work single row stripes or odd numbers of rows in different colors.
• Circular needles can be used two (or more) together for pieces with large numbers of stitches.

Circular needles do have a few disadvantages, however.

• It is difficult to measure the length of the work while it is on the needle.
• It is not possible to work intarsia in the round.
• Circular needles can be awkward to use when working short-row shaping.

EXPERT TIP

66 Use up your odd balls of yarn by making a striped scarf. Cast on twice as many stitches as your finished width then knit in the round, joining on and breaking off colors at random. There will be no ends to darn in since they will be hidden inside the scarf. 99

Question 85:
How do I join work after casting on with a circular needle?

Before casting on, straighten out the cord of your needle as much as possible. Nylon cords seem to "fix" into a tight curve in the packet. Immerse them in hot water for a few minutes and then straighten them out as much as you can between the fingers.

When you have cast on the required number of stitches make sure that they are not twisted around the needle. Once you have begun knitting with twisted stitches you will not be able to untwist them and will end up with a mobius loop.

Once you are sure that the stitches lie straight, bring the needle round so that the working yarn is at the right tip, and knit what was your slipknot from the tip of the left needle. This will be the first stitch of the initial row. Pull the yarn fairly firmly as you close the circle at the beginning of this row, then continue to knit the stitches, working counterclockwise, and without turning the work at any point.

BELOW Stitches cast on and ready to be joined into a circle.

Question 86:
How do I know which is the start of a round?

It can be easy to continue knitting around and around and forget which was the beginning of the round. This may not matter unless you need to work any shaping. If you didn't mark the beginning of the round with a stitch marker when you started, look for the tail end of yarn at the beginning of your cast-on row and follow the line of that stitch up through the knitting. Place a marker before it now!

If you are working in a multicolored or a distinct stitch pattern you will notice that you have a slight step or jog at one point in the knitting, or you will have two purl stitches together where you expected only one. The last stitch of Round two will appear to lie alongside the first stitch of Round three. This is the point where a new round begins.

Question 87:
How do I know what length of needle to use?

It is possible to work any number of stitches on any length of needle by pulling out a loop of the cord about halfway around, knitting as far as the loop and then pulling out another loop further on. But this is awkward, and can spoil the appearance of the stitches by stretching them.

Circular needles now come in such a wide variety of lengths that it is easier to match them to the number of stitches. The stitches should move comfortably along the needles without having to be stretched, and they should not be crammed on so tightly that they are in danger of falling off the tips. The fewer stitches you have to the inch the less you will be able to fit on the needle. Whatever the diameter of the needle—in other words, its stated size—the length should be at least 4 inches (10 cm) shorter than the finished circumference of the knitting. A rough guide to the minimum number of stitches various needle lengths can accommodate without overstretching them is given in the table below.

BELOW The white section shows the minimum number of stitches of each gauge that can be worked on a specific length of needle.

Length of needle	No of stitches to 1"			
	5	6	7	8
16"	80	120	150	180
24"	100	150	180	220
30"	115	170	210	250
36"	130	190	240	290

Question 88:

How do I avoid a long stitch between the needles when working on a set of double-pointed needles?

If you only require a few stitches on the needles then it is better to use more than three to hold the stitches, rather than trying to stretch them across a gap. At the start of each new needle, hold it behind the previous one. If this does not cure the problem and you are not working a complex pattern, after a few rounds move three or four of the stitches from the end of one needle to their neighboring needle. Continue for several more rounds then move some along again.

This method will not work if you have to perform any shaping on specified stitches—for example, at each side of a seam stitch on a sock—unless you move enough stitches to be able to work the shapings correctly. It can also be tricky on lace patterns.

It can help to pull the yarn firmly, working the first two stitches of each needle more tightly than the others. You can also try using five needles instead of four.

Question 89:
How do I work garter stitch on a circular needle?

Personally, I would prefer to work garter stitch on straight needles, as one of the advantages of knitting on circular needles is that, to form stockinette stitch, every row is a knit row. This is negated when working garter stitch in the round, as alternate rows have to be purled! But if you really hate to sew up and don't mind working lots of purl rows, then that is the way to do it.

Any stitch pattern that can be worked on two needles can also be worked on four or more or on a circular needle. If you are adapting a printed pattern that was made for two needles, remember that many stitch patterns will have extra edge stitches added in flat knitting so that pieces can be matched at the side seams. Ribs will often have an extra stitch or pair of stitches at the end to balance the pattern, but this is not necessary when knitting in the round.

Lace patterns can prove a little trickier to adapt, as they will often have half a pattern at the edges in order to center the design. In this case it is helpful to know how many stitches there are in a full repeat. If this is not stated in the pattern, count the number of stitches between asterisks where these are provided as a starting point for each group of stitches that form a pattern.

ABOVE Working purl in the normal way.

ABOVE Working purl by tensioning the yarn with the left thumb.

RIGHT Picot edge, stockinette, and garter stitch worked together on a circular needle.

Question 90:
How do I turn the heel of a sock?

There are different ways of making a heel, but they all involve working on only a portion of the stitches. The method, shown below, will form a square and is known as a "Dutch heel."

The stitches are divided in half, with one set being left for the instep and the other used for the heel. The heel stitches are worked back and forth on two needles with a slip stitch at each end of the row until it forms a square. To check if it is square fold it back along the diagonal; the stitches on the needle should match the length of the side edge. When the square is complete work across two-thirds of the stitches, for example:

HOW IT'S DONE

Row 1 Knit 20, then slip 1, knit 1, pass slipped stitch over and turn the work, ready to begin the short purl row.
Row 2 Purl 10, then purl 2 together, turn.
Row 3 Knit 10, slip 1, knit 1, pass slipped stitch over, turn.
Row 4 As Row 2.
Row 5 As Row 3.

Repeat Rows 2 and 3 until all stitches are worked off, then knit one row on the remaining stitches. Pick up and knit stitches down the side of the heel. Using another needle, knit the instep stitches left on the other two needles. Using a third needle, pick up and knit stitches along the other side of the heel. Arrange the stitches evenly around the needles so that the heel will come at the center back, and then continue in rounds, decreasing one stitch at each side of the instep until the number of stitches is the same as were cast on. Continue until the foot is long enough, minus approximately 2 inches (5 cm) for the toe. Divide the stitches onto two needles and decrease at each end of both needles on alternate rounds until there is approximately half the number of stitches you started with. Graft these stitches together.

Harris County Public Library
HCPL Jacinto City
06/20/12 01:14PM

To renew call: 713-747-4763
or visit: www.hcpl.net
You must have your library card number
and pin number to renew.

PATRON: GANN CAROLYN JEAN

Ghost wolf of Thunder Mountain : frontier
CALL NO: Henry W-SS
 34028039472999
DUE: 07/05/12

Knitting : 200 Q & A : questions answered
CALL NO: 746.432 Tay
 34028067356460
DUE: 07/05/12

TOTAL: 2

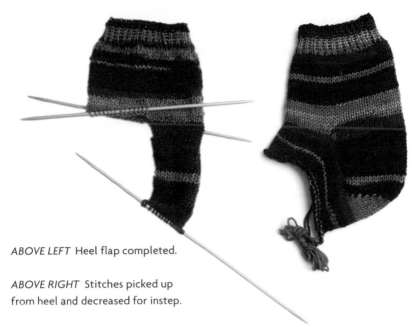

ABOVE LEFT Heel flap completed.

ABOVE RIGHT Stitches picked up from heel and decreased for instep.

Question 91:
How do I avoid a step, or jog, at the beginning of a round?

If you are working in stockinette or garter stitch this step will not be noticeable, but certain patterns will have an obvious jump between rounds that can spoil the appearance of the finished work. If you are working a definite pattern or rows of stripes that have become misaligned, after you have worked your first two rounds slip the first stitch of the next round instead of knitting it. On subsequent rounds the step should be less noticeable, but if it should become obvious, slip it again.

You can also try knitting the first stitch of a new round with both colors and then pulling the one you do not want more tightly so that it disappears behind the correct one. Alternatively, at the end of the round, lift the first stitch of the row below and knit it together with your next stitch. Repeat this on every alternate row.

Question 92:
What is the method of making a traditional guernsey?

The basic guernsey shape has remained the same for many years. It was always intended as a working garment and is typically loose and square to allow freedom of movement and ease of repair. It is traditionally knitted in navy five-ply wool on fine needles—size 0 (2 mm) being the most common—with about 12 stitches and 20 rounds to the inch. For a firm edge, stitches are often cast on with the yarn doubled, or sometimes a knotted edge is used, which is decorative and hardwearing. The knitting is continued with single yarn and worked in the round as far as the armholes, often with a purl stitch to mark the position where seams would be.

Gussets are made at the underarm within this seam to eliminate any "pull" on the area, and the work is divided for the back and front, which are worked separately on two needles. There is little if any neck shaping, but wide bands of knitting known as straps are often added at the shoulders to give extra width. These straps are often patterned and are sometimes continued down the

BELOW Traditional guernsey shape worked in the round from the bottom upward. Sleeves worked downward after body is completed.

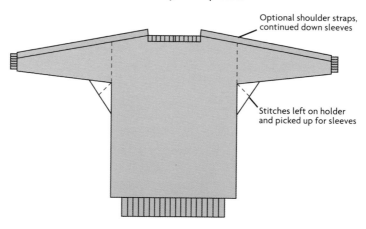

Optional shoulder straps, continued down sleeves

Stitches left on holder and picked up for sleeves

sleeves. The rest of the stitches for the sleeve are picked up from the armhole edge and gusset stitches; they are then worked from the top downward, which has the added bonus of making them easy to repair where the saltwater and general wear and tear causes them to fray.

A neckband is usually knitted fairly loosely and may be finished with two rows of ridges or a short ribbed band. Some Scottish patterns will have tighter neckbands with buttons at the side.

This square-shaped garment can be adapted to all forms of knitting. It is typical of Fair Isle garments, which again were originally intended as work clothing. Steeks (see below) were added at the armholes, and where shaping was required to facilitate knitting these multicolored garments completely in the round.

Question 93:
What are "steeks"?

Steek is a relatively modern word for a technique used in the Shetland Islands for carrying colors across openings while continuing to knit in the round. They are used mainly at armhole edges so that the back and fronts don't have to be knitted separately back and forth.

To knit a steek, cast on about ten extra stitches at the start of the armhole. Knit these stitches alternately in the same colors you are using in that round. If you are changing colors in a round, change them in the middle of the steek. Before picking up the stitches for a sleeve, cut through the steek at the center point. Pick up the stitches from the inner, or body, edge of the steek and work the sleeve downward. When it is finished, trim back the steek to two or three stitches and oversew it to the inside of the armhole.

Cardigan fronts and V-necked openings can be treated in the same way.

An alternative method of creating a steek is simply to wrap both yarns being used around the needle a few times before commencing each round; remove the wrapped yarn from the preceding round each time, leaving it to form a long ladder. These ends must then be trimmed and darned in when the work is finished.

Question 94:
What is a seam stitch?

A seam stitch is placed where a sewn seam would be if pieces were knitted flat and not in the round. It is a useful device for marking the side stitches of a guernsey in order to place the gussets correctly, or to mark the position where the work should be divided for the back and front. It can also give the piece a better shape by not ballooning out so much at the sides.

Working one purl stitch usually makes a seam stitch, but sometimes the seams are made more obvious by working several stitches, in purl, moss stitch, or rib. One seam stitch will be placed above the first cast-on stitch, and the other will be halfway along from this point.

Question 95:
How do I make an underarm gusset?

The underarm gusset is diamond shaped, just less than 3 inches (8 cm) across at its widest point, and is usually knitted throughout in stocking stitch, although it is also found in moss stitch and its variations, or in single rib. It is started from the seam stitch, about 3 inches (8 cm) short of the armhole shaping. Increase twice in the seam stitch to make three stitches out of one. Stitches are then gradually increased at each edge of the gusset itself on alternate rows or less

RIGHT **Stitches of gusset left on waste yarn.**

frequently, until it is about 3 inches (8 cm) wide; enough to give freedom of movement at the underarm.

At this point, when the work is ready to divide for the armhole, the stitches are left on a holder until they are picked up as part of the sleeve. The extra stitches are then gradually decreased at the same rate as before until just one stitch remains for the underarm seam stitch. The sleeve is shaped by decreasing as frequently as necessary on each side of this seam stitch.

Question 96:
How do I make a square "in the round"?

Various shapes can be made in the round, including squares. The most obvious method is to use the number of double-pointed needles that corresponds to the number of sides of your shape; in other words, four for a square, five for a pentagon, and so on, as this makes it easier to see where to place the increases.

To begin a square, cast on two stitches for each side and knit the first round. Second round: increase in every stitch. Third and every alternate round: knit straight. Fourth round: increase at the beginning and end of each needle.

Repeat rounds three and four until your square is big enough.

The number of rounds knitted straight will vary for different shapes, and it is usually a matter of trial and error how many straight rounds are required to keep the shape flat.

If you find it cumbersome to cast on a few stitches to each needle, either cast them all onto one and then divide them between the others, or, crochet a length of chain corresponding to the number of stitches required. Join it into a ring with a slip stitch, then pick up and knit the back strand of each chain until the required number are on the first needle. Continue with the second needle, and so on, until all the chains have been used.

7 WORKING IN COLOR

Items created with multicolored knitting always look spectacular, yet they are no more difficult to achieve than knitting with a single color.

Question 97:
How do I knit multicolored patterns?

Knitting horizontal stripes into a design is the easiest way of introducing color. Vary the number of rows in each color to make the design more interesting, remembering that if you want to work odd numbers of rows you will need to use a circular needle or a long double-pointed one. Slip some of the stitches to break the straight lines, or knit a few rows between each stripe in alternate colors for each stitch. For a more dramatic look work zig-zag stripes by increasing and decreasing across the row.

More complicated multicolor designs are made using intarsia, Fair Isle, or mosaic knitting techniques. You will normally need to follow a chart of some kind to knit these designs, although many vintage patterns gave only stitch-by-stitch instructions. If you are using one of these, it is sometimes easier to follow if you can convert it to a chart yourself.

Some cross stitch patterns can be used for knitting, but they are made on squared paper and can look squashed if followed exactly. Knitted stitches are usually wider than they are high, so you may need to add a row or two within the design if this can be accommodated. Rectangular paper is available for charting knitting designs but it is simple enough to make your own using appropriate computer programs.

Question 98:
How do I stop the yarns from tangling?

This is a question that occurs time and again and one that has never been solved properly. But there are ways of reducing the tangles.

• Turn the work clockwise at the end of the knit rows and counterclockwise at the end of the purl rows.
• Do not twist the yarns together at color changes unless you must.

- Keep the yarns in different jars or boxes arranged around your feet.
- Use short lengths of yarn and pull them free of each other as they start to tangle.
- Use bobbins* kept close up to the work.
- Break off any colors that you won't be using for a few rows.
- Keep your main yarn in the right hand and use your left hand for the contrast yarn. You can do this vice versa, but be consistent.

   * You can purchase bobbins, use cardboard, or just make a butterfly (by wrapping yarn in a figure eight around your thumb and index finger).

ABOVE A selection of bobbins: finger-wound yarn (top); homemade card bobbin (middle); proprietary bobbin (bottom).

Question 99:
How should I hold the yarns?

There are several ways of working with two yarns at once. Try different methods and find the one that is most comfortable for you.

   The simplest method is to drop the first color and pick up the second, letting go of them each time, but this method can be slow. To speed up the process try holding the main yarn in the usual way and the contrast yarn over the middle finger of your right hand. Alternatively, hold the main yarn in your usual way and hold the contrast yarn over your left index or middle finger. This is a combination of English and Continental methods of holding the yarn.

   To practice holding both yarns together, try knitting stitches in alternate colors. Cast on about 40 stitches with your main color and knit one round. Next round: knit one main, one contrast to the end of the round. Next round: knit one contrast, one main to the end of the round. Repeat these two rounds several times until you become accustomed to working with both colors at once.

Question 100:
What is the difference between intarsia and Jacquard?

Intarsia is used for working large blocks of color—often on a plain background as in picture knitting. There can be several colors in a row and each color is a separate length of yarn. None of the colors is carried across the row as they are in Jacquard designs. Where the colors change over, the yarns are twisted around one another to prevent holes forming. The yarn is not stranded across the back of the work, therefore there is only a single thickness of fabric.

Because of the nature of working with each color picked up from its finishing point and worked back to the other side of the design, intarsia can not be knitted in the round; the yarns would not be in the correct place for the next block of color. Some parts of the design, where there are only a few stitches to be worked in a particular color, can be duplicate stitched.

Jacquard can be worked in the round as it is worked across the row. The yarns are carried from beginning to end and stranded or woven in as appropriate. This produces a double thickness of fabric. The designs can be geometric or stylized natural forms similar to those found in cross stitch.

In both instances, some of the stitches can be in pattern rather than stockinette.

ABOVE An intarsia design (left); Jacquard (right).

Question 101:
What is the difference between Fair Isle and intarsia?

Fair Isle is a specific form of Jacquard with its own characteristic patterns. It is always worked in stockinette, and garments are traditionally knitted in the round to the basic guernsey shape. There are only ever two colors used in a round, and the patterns are usually geometric. Ideally, there should be no more than five stitches between color changes because the yarn is stranded across the back and not woven in. Stranding across more than five stitches produces awkward floats.

Fair Isle knitting is instantly recognizable by the bands of pattern that change shape and color throughout the length of the piece. A broad band of pattern worked over several rows is usually followed by a narrow band known as a "peerie." There are numerous designs for these with just a few stitches and rows to each shape.

The single contrast colors that are carried across the back of the work make the garment soft and pliable, unlike some forms of intarsia that can be stiff where a number of colors are woven in. True

Fair Isle knitting is carried out with Shetland yarn of approximately worsted or finer weight. Early Fair Isle garments followed the basic "guernsey" shape, knitted entirely in the round with extra stitches or wraps of yarn added at the start of the armhole or the center front of a cardigan. These would be cut through and sewn down later, after the stitches had been picked up.

ABOVE A Fair Isle design.

Question 102:
When should I "strand" and when should I "weave"?

Stranding, that is carrying the yarn not in use across the back of the work, should only be used for five or less stitches. If there are more than this in a block of color then some will have to be woven in.

* Knit two stitches as normal, then lift the non-working color onto the tip of the right-hand needle before knitting it as though it were part of the stitch. Let the strand fall back behind the working color, and continue with the main color only for another one or two stitches. Repeat from *, keeping the floats loose but not slack until you are ready to take up the next color.

If you need to weave in your main color rather than the contrast then the technique is a little more awkward.

Insert the right needle into the stitch, wind the non-working yarn around the needle as if to knit it, then wind the working yarn around the needle in the usual way. Take the non-working yarn back behind the working yarn, and complete the knitted stitch.

Stranding and weaving can also be done on purl rows where necessary.

Question 103:
What are slip-stitch patterns?

These can be used to work a simple form of color knitting. Only one color is used at a time in each row.

The first color is used for two rows, then the second color is taken up for the next two. Any number of different colors can be used, and there is no need to carry them along the row, nor to strand or weave in. Patterns are usually worked with the yarn at the back of the slipped stitches on the knit rows and at the front of them on the purl rows, but there is no reason why the yarn should not pass across the right side of the work for a different effect. Slip the stitches purlwise so that they have the same appearance as the knit stitches and do not appear twisted.

Multicolored slip-stitch patterns have advantages over other forms of color knitting in that yarns do not get tangled and many different textures and weights of yarn can be used in the same piece.

Question 104:
What are "floats"?

Floats are the strands left at the back of the work when changing colors. They should not be too long—no more than 1 inch (2.5 cm) —as they can cause an uneven tension, or catch in the fingers.

If they are left too long for the number of stitches that they cross, the stitch at the beginning and end of the float will become large and loose. If they are too short they will draw up the work, giving a pleated effect sometimes seen in tea cozy patterns.

It makes the fabric more even if long strands are woven in every few stitches. And if the same color is always carried across the top of the other color, the contrast stitches should not show on the right side of the work. When knitting with two colors, carry them both right to the end of the row and twist them together at the edge to keep the first few stitches even.

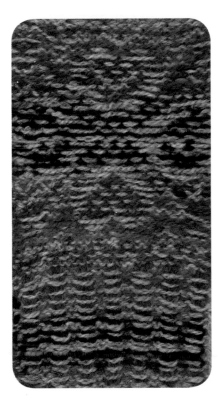

ABOVE Short floats on the back of a piece of Fair Isle.

Question 105:
What is "mosaic knitting"?

This is a form of slip-stitch knitting based on geometric patterns and using a combination of knit and purl stitches. The slipped stitches are often worked in garter stitch, and because it takes two rows of knitting to make one pattern row, it can be slow to grow!

Patterns are worked from charts with each line representing two rows, because the second row is simply a repeat of the first.

It is more difficult to describe than it is to do. The sample was worked in a Greek key pattern over 26 stitches with color A for the first two rows and color B for the

next two. Repeat the sequence and frequency of changing colors throughout the pattern; repeat the stitches following the * on each row and knit any leftover stitches at the end as instructed.

HOW IT'S DONE

Rows 1 and 2 Knit.
Rows 2 and 4 Knit 1,* slip 1, knit 5 to end, knit 1.
Rows 5 and 6 Knit 2,* slip 1, knit 3, slip 1, knit 1, to end.
Rows 1 and 8 Knit 1, * slip 1, knit 3, slip 1, knit 1, to end.
Rows 2 and 10 Knit 6, * slip 1, knit 5, to end, knit 2.
Rows 11 and 12 As Rows 1 and 2.
Rows 13 and 14 Knit 4, * slip 1, knit 5, to end, slip 1, knit 3.
Rows 15 and 16 * Knit 3, slip 1, knit 1, slip 1, to end, knit 2.
Rows 17 and 18 Knit 2, * slip 1, knit 1, slip 1, knit 3, to end.
Rows 19 and 20 Knit 3, * slip 1, knit 5, to end, slip 1, knit 4.

RIGHT Simple Fair Isle pattern used as a border.

Question 106:
How do I work multicolored rib?

Many Fair Isle designs have multicolored ribbing, sometimes known as corrugated rib. It is usually worked as knit two, purl two, with all the knit stitches in the main color, and the colors of the purl stitches changed as frequently as you wish to match the body of the garment.

Sometimes this sequence is reversed; all the knit stitches are worked in changing colors while the purl stitches are worked throughout in one color, usually the same as the background color of the first few rows of the body. As with any item knitted in the round, any number of rows of each color can be worked.

If you are working in the round, return the contrast yarns to the back of the knitting after working the purl stitches and do not pull them too tightly. If you are knitting back and forth, always strand the yarns across the main color on the wrong side. Because of these strands of yarn, the rib will not be as elastic as that worked in one color throughout.

BELOW Knit stitches are in main color; purl stitches are in contrast color.

Question 107:
How do I avoid a broken stripe when changing color on the purl stitches?

This is the same effect that you get on the reverse side of stockinette or if you change to a different color on the wrong side of a garter stitch row. The ridge will be a mix of the two colors, and if it is on the right side of the work both of these colors will show. Knitting is formed from a continuous thread that weaves itself in and out of the stitches that have already been formed. The back of the stitch, the ridged side, will be hidden behind the smooth part of it, and so any change of color will not show on the smooth side. If you study the way a stitch is formed you will understand why this is so. Follow the shape of the stitches with a needle and some contrast colored yarn and it will be easier to see how this works.

Some designers use this feature to create a more gentle transition from one color to another, and on Fair Isle garments it is perfectly acceptable as one of the traditional methods of working. If you want to eliminate it, work the first row of a change of color as all knit. Or use one of the alternative methods of working a multicolored rib as described opposite; work the knit stitches on the right side in different colors and keep to one color for the purl stitches. Again, the rib will be less elastic than one worked in the same color throughout.

EXPERT TIP

❝ For a subtle changeover effect try working with two different colors held together. After a few rows take a third color and replace one of the original colors with this for a few more rows. Replace the second color with a fourth color, and so on, for a gradual change of shades. ❞

Question 108:
Why do my stitches look uneven when I work in color?

If you usually have an even tension when working stockinette there is no reason why this should not be maintained as you become more familiar with working in color. Practice holding the yarns in different ways and knitting with alternate colors across the row; **A**, **B** alternately on row one, then **B**, **A** alternately on row two. Try knitting back and forth as well as with circular needles. You may find that the latter method suits you better as you do not have to make any purl stitches. Purl stitches are often a little looser than knit stitches, and some people adjust for this by working with a size smaller needle on the purl rows.

Be consistent with the way you hold the yarn as this will ensure that, as you change color, A always passes over **B**. Your stitches will look uneven if **B** sometimes passes above **A**, and one color will form larger stitches than the other. If you are relaxed and comfortable when you knit, your stitches will be the same. But in any case, they have a way of equalizing themselves in wear, and older garments often look much neater than new ones!

BELOW Some distorted stitches at the center, where the yarn is woven in.

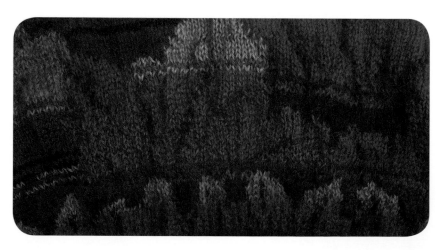

Question 109:
Why does the fabric look distorted when I do multicolored knitting?

The strands that lie across the back of the fabric must lie straight across the stitches that they span. You may be pulling too tightly on them without being aware of it. After you have knitted a few stitches, gently but firmly slide them along the needle, opening them out. Knit your next few stitches and repeat the process. The strands should now lie straight and flat across the back of the work. If you are working on circulars the stitches have a tendency to slide back, since the cord is much thinner than the points of the needles, but the more times you pull on them the more they will even out. If you are working on double-pointed needles you are probably in the habit of tightening up the yarn for the first stitch of each needle, but avoid doing this in stranded knitting if you find that your work is beginning to pucker.

BELOW Strands pulled tightly across parts of the back, causing the work to pucker. Other strands have been left loose to be darned in later.

Question 110:
Should I break off yarns or carry them up the side of the work?

If you are working stripes of just a few rows each time, and provided the yarn is not too thick, carrying them up the side of the work will be less time-consuming and the result will look relatively neat. After every inch (2.5 cm) or so, wrap the working yarn around the other yarn ends so that there are no long floats at the sides. If you are working with anything thicker than knitting worsted/DK and all the color changes are at one edge—for example, at the front of a cardigan—this edge may not measure the same as that of the other front because of the extra bulk. It will also be difficult to pick up and knit stitches for a horizontal button band, so consider changing colors at the opposite end—bearing in mind that you will then have two lots of floats in that seam—in other words, two lots of strands running up the side edge of the seam, one from the front piece and one from the back.

If you are having problems getting your seams to match, or if you are working wider stripes and there are large gaps between each change of color, then it is better to break off the yarns and darn in the ends later. After you have sewn the seams together weave the yarn up through five or six stitches along the extreme edge of the seam, across through half a stitch, and then back down through the other half of the same few stitches.

If the edges are not going to be seamed, on a scarf, for example, weave the yarn through its own color, this time passing it diagonally under five or six stitches, and then back through the adjacent stitches.

EXPERT TIP

66 If you are working wide stripes where the carried yarn would form long loops, knit both colors together at the beginning of the round, pulling on the non-working one afterward so that it becomes hidden behind the stitch. 99

Question 111:
How do I follow a chart?

This is a very simple chart showing how a row of lozenge shapes such as that found in a peerie pattern is created in a contrasting color from the one used for the background.

The numbers in the left-hand column denote the rows; the numbers along the bottom denote the stitches. Stitch 1.1 is worked in the background color and stitch 2.1 is in the contrast color, as is stitch 6.1, and so on along the row.

On the next row, if you were working back and forth on two needles, you would begin with stitch 20 on row 2. Stitch 20.2 is worked in the background color, then 19.2 is worked in the contrast, and so on. In other words, you need to read the chart in reverse, from left to right, for the purl rows. This does not apply when you are working in the round, as the right side of the work is always facing you and every round is read from right to left.

Row 4 is the last row of this chart and from that point the work is completed in the background color alone, unless the pattern gives instructions to repeat the chart at a later stage.

All charts are based on the same principles, with one square for each stitch. Some will use symbols, as in this case, and others will use a color. Some publications will show the layout of the design in chart form over the whole item, with shapings and different sizes also superimposed on the chart. Where a pattern is composed of a number of repeats of certain stitches, only the portion of the design that is repeated may be drawn. Instructions for the number of repeats required in each piece for each size will be given in the written instructions. In the chart below, the design actually repeats over four stitches while the rest of the stitches are merely a repetition of these. The chart could actually have been drawn for these four stitches only, but the whole chart is shown in order to clarify the instructions.

	20	19	18	17	16	15	14	13	12	11	10	9	8	7	6	5	4	3	2	1
4			x				x				x				x				x	
3		x		x		x		x		x		x		x		x		x		x
2		x		x		x		x		x		x		x		x		x		x
1			x				x				x				x				x	

Question 112:
What do I do if the color I want next is at the wrong end of the row?

If you are working single rows or uneven numbers of rows in contrast colors you will need to use at least three different colors and work so that you are ready to pick up the required color from the correct place. There are mathematical formulas for working this out, and you need to plan the sequence before you start. Otherwise just let the stripes work where they will, and pick up the color that is in the correct place for the next row!

If you are following a pattern and you are left with the yarn at the wrong end of the work you can

• break it off and rejoin for the beginning of the next row.
• use separate balls of yarn for each change of color.
• use double-pointed or circular needles for certain rows.

If you decide to use the third option, slide the stitches to the other end of the needle, to where your required color is, then knit that row in the same direction as your last one. You may sometimes have to purl two rows, one after the other, if you are working in stockinette.

EXPERT TIP

❝ If your edges are not going to be hidden in a seam, try covering them with I-cord. Cast on three or four stitches and as you knit each row work the last stitch together with one from your main piece of knitting. ❞

Question 113:
How do I stop a gap forming between the stitches when working vertical stripes?

This can often be a problem when working intarsia, or picture knitting. Each block of color uses a separate ball of yarn, therefore any stitches that are always vertically arranged will not be linked to a preceding stitch. To stop the gap forming between them, the yarns must be twisted together.

You can either drop the old color and pick up the new color from underneath the first one or, if you are holding both yarns at the same time, lay color **A** along the left-hand needle and then lift color **B** up over it before knitting the next stitch. Color **A** will drop back into place and be caught by color **B**. The yarns should form a vertical line of stitches, resembling back stitches, along the back of the work.

Where the vertical line breaks and becomes a diagonal, there is no need to twist the stitches on every row. They will be linked automatically as the color moves across its neighboring stitch.

BELOW In the lower portion of the sample the two yarns are not twisted together, so there is a gap between color changes.

Question 114:
How do I carry the colors along the row when working argyle socks?

Argyle socks are made to resemble Scottish tartan, but worked in a diamond, instead of a square, pattern. The diamonds are of different colors bisected by diagonal lines. Every shape, including the diagonal lines, must have its own ball of color and these have to be twisted together on alternate rows as described on page 127. They cannot be carried along the row because then they would be in the wrong position for the next row.

Because of the arrangement of the pattern argyle socks have to be knitted on two needles and seamed down the back of the leg. If they were knitted in the round the color would be in the wrong place for the start of the next row. To save carrying some of the colors, the bisecting lines of the diamonds can be duplicate stitched (Swiss darned) after the sock is finished.

Question 115:
What is unique about Sanquhar knitting?

Sanquhar, in Dumfriesshire, Scotland, is noted for its particular form of knitting, mainly of gloves and mittens. They were knitted in fine three-ply wool to a firm gauge using two colors. The most popular types were black and white or dark brown and natural, sometimes with the cuffs lined in a bright red, which would show at the edge. While this type of knitting is known as Sanquhar, similar items were also made in Cumbria, England, usually in natural and brown rather than black and white.

The cuffs themselves were knitted in a multicolored rib, often followed by a band containing the initials of the owner. The patterns on the hand would then be based on a geometric design, sometimes

Renewal Slip

Harris County Public Library
HCPL Jacinto City
06/20/12 01:15PM

****

PATRON: GANN CAROLYN JEAN

Due Date: 07/19/12
CALL NO: Henry W-SS
Barcode: 34028039472999
Ghost wolf of Thunder Mountain : frontier stories /

Due Date: 07/19/12
CALL NO: 746.432 Tay
Barcode: 34028067356460
Knitting : 200 Q & A : questions answered on everything from casting on to deco

Total: 2

LEFT Example of Sanquhar patterns

Duke's pattern

Midge and fly

Shepherd's plaid

of alternate stitches in dark and light and sometimes a more elaborate one of diamonds or saltires within squares, or dark and light "speckled" diamonds, popularly known as shepherd's plaid. The patterns may have developed from other textiles in the area, notably the weaving of checks and plaids. On some gloves the fingers would be knitted in a different pattern again, possibly one of the smaller ones such as "midge and fly," where a speckled pattern is interspersed with the smallest possible cross.

While some of the patterns appear similar to those of argyle socks, Sanquhar patterns can be knitted in the round as only two colors are used throughout.

CABLES AND TWISTS

There are literally hundreds of variations on
cable patterns; working stitches out of sequence
using a cable needle creates them all.

Question 116:
How do I make a cable?

Cables are made by crossing over two or more stitches so that the sequence in which they are worked is altered. In order to move the stitches they usually have to be held on a cable needle until they are next required.

The stitches to be moved are slipped from the left-hand needle onto the cable needle so that the next group of stitches can be knitted; in fact they, and those from the cable needle, could also be purled or worked in any other type of stitch. But the principle is the same whichever stitch you use and however many stitches you are moving.

Cables can also be made in groups, forming a braided effect, and sometimes more than one cable needle is used to move stitches in opposite directions. They can also be worked in more than one color and knitted in the round as well as flat.

It is possible to work cables without an extra needle by lifting the stitches to be knitted last onto the right needle and then transferring them in the correct order to the left needle. This technique works best on wool yarns and is not to be recommended for yarns like silk or rayon, which are much too slippery.

ABOVE Stitches held on cable needle at front.

ABOVE Completed cable.

Question 117:
How do I make a cable cross in a particular direction?

To form the design the stitches on the cable needle are held either at the front or at the back of the work. If they are held at the front with the right side of the work facing you, the crossed stitches will move toward the left.

To make a basic four-stitch rope cable that crosses to the left on a background of reverse stockinette see below.

To make the stitches cross to the right, perform a similar operation but hold the cable needle with its stitches at the back of the work.

By combining these basic principles a variety of complex-looking cable patterns can be formed.

ABOVE **Left and right crossed cables.**

HOW IT'S DONE

Row 1 Purl 2, knit 4 (these 4 will be the cabled stitches), purl 2.
Row 2 Knit 2, purl 4, knit 2.
Row 3 Purl 2, slip the next 2 stitches onto a cable needle and hold it at the front of the work, knit the next 2 stitches from the left-hand needle, knit the 2 stitches from the cable needle, purl 2.
Row 4 As row 2.
Repeat these four rows.

Question 118:
How do I work a braided cable?

In order to make the cable appear braided the stitches must be divided into groups, which are worked alternately in different directions.

In the sample, which was worked on a moss-stitch background, the cable was made as follows.

HOW IT'S DONE

Cast on 24 stitches.
Row 1 (Knit 1, purl 1) 3 times, knit 12, (knit 1, purl 1) 3 times.
Row 2 (Purl 1, knit 1) 3 times, purl 12, (purl 1, knit 1) 3 times.
Row 3 (Knit 1, purl 1) 3 times, slip the next 3 onto a cable needle and hold at the back of the work, knit 3, then knit 3 from the cable needle, repeat this cable again, (knit 1, purl 1) 3 times.
Row 4 As Row 2.
Row 5 As Row 1.
Row 6 As Row 2.
Row 7 (Knit 1, purl 1) 3 times, knit 3, slip the next 3 onto the cable needle and hold at the front, knit 3, then knit 3 from cable needle, knit 3, (knit 1, purl 1) 3 times.
Row 8 As Row 2.

Repeat Rows 1–8 to form the plaited cable.

Question 119:
What is the difference between a cable and a twist?

Twists are usually only worked over two stitches at once, and don't need any tools other than your two needles (or one if you are working on a circular needle). They don't have much effect on the gauge of your pattern and they are fairly quick to work. Like cables, they can also be made to form a plaited effect by alternating the direction in which they cross on each right side row. The result is similar to basket weaving. Twists can also form a mock cable by lifting one slipped stitch in front of the next two or three.

Cables are worked over several stitches at once, and work best with a third needle to transfer the stitches to their working position. This can be a little more time-consuming than twisting the stitches, although some people will work cables without the use of the extra needle by lifting the crossing stitches off the right-hand needle and holding them in their fingers, then replacing the stitches in their new order onto the left-hand needle. If you try this don't attempt to hold too many stitches at once, as it is awkward trying to slip them back onto the needle without

dropping any. This method can also cause the stitches to stretch too much, and some yarns will actually break as the stitches are being moved from one needle to the other!

EXPERT TIP

66 Twisted stitches will stand out equally well on a stockinette background, whereas cables look best if worked between purl stitches. They will look even more prominent if the top stitch is worked through the back. 99

Question 120:
How do I twist, or cross, stitches?

Twisted stitches are like miniature cables; they are knitted out of sequence but this time without using a cable needle, as they are only worked over two stitches at a time. Again, like cables, they can be made to move in different directions; to move to the right the first stitch must pass behind the second, and vice versa. Stitches that have been twisted can also be moved again on subsequent rows as can be seen in the illustration.

There are different ways of crossing the stitches:

• Insert the right needle into the front of the second stitch and knit it without removing it from the left-hand needle, then knit the first stitch and slip both stitches off the needle.
• Insert the right needle into the back of the second stitch and knit it, then knit the first stitch.
• Insert the right needle into the second stitch, lift it over the first stitch and knit it, then knit the first stitch.

• Knit two together without removing them from the needle, insert the right needle into the first stitch and knit it, then slip both stitches off together. Similar methods are used for purl stitches.

ABOVE Stitches twisted in different directions.

Question 121:
Why has the cabled section of my sweater come out tighter than the stockinette section?

Cables are worked over a combination of knit and purl stitches like ribbing, so this section of the work will appear narrower than stockinette. But cabling is also less elastic, since working stitches out of sequence means that the yarn can no longer stretch widthways. Consequently it is necessary to add extra stitches where the cables appear. One stitch for every four stitches of cable is usually enough. If the cable pattern is to begin immediately after the ribbing it is fairly simple to increase on the last ribbed row. For a neater finish place the increases carefully so that some of the plain stitches can be carried up into the cables, even if this means that the stitches are not increased evenly across the row.

Where the cables are worked in the body of the garment, either singly or in groups, increase in the cable on the first crossing row. For example, if you are designing a sweater that introduces a new six-stitch rope cable every few rows, following the instructions below.

HOW IT'S DONE

Row 1 Work to position of cable, purl 2, knit 5, purl 2, work to end.
Row 2 Work to position of cable, knit 2, purl 5, knit 2, work to end.
Row 3 Work to position of cable, purl 2, slip 3 onto cable needle, increase in 1st stitch on left-hand needle, knit 1, knit 3 from cable needle, purl 2, work to end.
Row 4 On subsequent rows, work stitches as established.

Repeat the increases each time a new cable is introduced, and remember to make any corresponding decreases where the cables end, including during the bind-off row.

Question 122:
How do I count the rows between cables?

Cables are usually worked over a regular number of rows, for instance a right cross will be made on every sixth row. The most accurate way to count these repeats is by using a row counter or by making a mark on your pattern for each row that you finish.

But because it is sometimes difficult to see which row the cable was actually crossed on, simply count the rows in another part of the pattern, where there are no cables. Tie a piece of colored yarn to one of the edge stitches the first time you make a cable. Count the rows from here to the stitches on your needle, which, incidentally, are also counted as a row. Divide this figure by the number of rows you work between repeats; if you have counted 68 rows and you are making a cable on every sixth row, dividing 68 by six will give you 11 with two over. You should have made cables 11 times so far and will need to work another four rows before your next cable.

BELOW An alternative method is to count the rows on the wrong side (shown here).

RIGHT Sweater trimmed with cables on collar and sleeves.

Question 123:
Why do I get an uneven stitch next to my cables?

All stitches have a natural pull; knit stitches pull lengthways and purl stitches pull widthways. If they are worked next to each other they will pull in opposite directions. When knit stitches are used in cables they are being pulled away from their natural inclination and will lose some of their elasticity. Loose stitches are especially noticeable when knitting cotton yarns, as they are not very elastic anyway.

If you are designing your own pattern, try using an uneven number of stitches in the cable groups, in other words, cross three over two. This way there will be less pull across the stitches.

Another reason for loose stitches is due to the order in which stitches are formed. Making a purl stitch after a knit stitch causes the yarn to travel further; it must be brought to the front and wrapped around the needle before making the stitch. This causes the adjacent knit stitch to look slightly larger as it, and not the purl stitch, takes up the slack when the stitch is released from the needle.

If you want to work cables without any purl stitches between, try leaving the stitches on safety pins or short stitch holders, then knitting them off on the following round.

Question 124:
How can I design an Aran sweater?

For your first attempt, choose a basic shape based on rectangles with dropped sleeves and a square neckline. That way you will have no increasing or decreasing to interrupt the stitch patterns. Once you have made your gauge swatch and worked out how many stitches and rows you require, it is a fairly simple matter to choose the designs you like and arrange them to fit your given number of stitches.

Use graph paper and place your main stitch pattern at the center front, marking the maximum width that it will take up on the appropriate row. Outline this group of stitches with a more simple design such as a six-stitch cable, leaving room for a few purl stitches in between. Leave a few more purl stitches and place a medium size design outside this cable, followed by a similar number of purl stitches. Either repeat the six-stitch cable or work another simple design followed by a set of moss stitch, rib, reverse stockinette, or trinity stitch (see

page 142) for the remainder of the stitches. If necessary, adjust the number of plain stitches between the different stitch patterns to fit in with your measurement.

When you reach the neck shaping, try to finish on a reasonable point of the pattern, adding a few extra rows if necessary. Stitch patterns do not have to contain the same number of rows between repeats; once you have your design worked out on graph paper it is easy to see the relationship between the different groups and where stitches should be crossed.

Question 125:
How do I work trinity stitch?

Trinity stitch, or blackberry stitch, is one of the traditional Aran stitches. It is sometimes used as a central panel and sometimes at the edges of a sweater. Trinity stitch is worked by increasing and decreasing alternating groups of stitches, and needs a multiple of four stitches. It is difficult, but not impossible, to work shaping over this stitch. If you need to decrease at the beginning and end of a row, work the first and last four stitches before you start the shaping as purl stitches. Make sure that the number of stitches worked in trinity stitch remains a

multiple of four each time. If you begin a row, or part of a row, with purl three together, you must end it with knit one, purl one, knit one in the last stitch or you will find that the number of stitches you have on the needles will not tally with the pattern instructions and will vary from row to row.

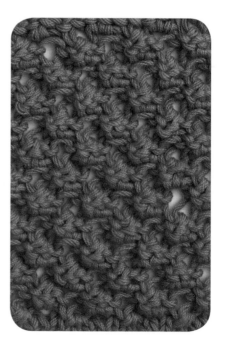

HOW IT'S DONE

Beginning with a purl row on the right side of the fabric:
Row 1 Purl.
Row 2 (Knit 1, purl 1, knit 1) all into next stitch, purl 3 together.
Row 3 Purl.
Row 4 Purl 3 together, (knit 1, purl 1, knit 1) all into next stitch.

Repeat these four rows.

Question 126:
What do I do about cables when I start shaping?

Just as with trinity stitch (see opposite), some adjustments may need to be made when working cables at armhole, neck edges, and so on. It often makes for a neater finish if that portion of the pattern is not cabled but continued in stockinette, or whichever stitch is used for the background. Carry on with the cable for as long as seems appropriate. At V-necks try to finish after a second or fourth row beyond a cable, and split it so that half travels along one side of the neckline and half on the other.

Decreasings can be worked within these stitches or outside them, working the other cables for as long as possible before continuing them without crossing. When you reach the point where you need to shape the shoulders, work enough rows after the last cable so that when the shoulders are joined they will have the same number of rows between the crossings as the rest of the garment. You may need to add or subtract a few rows before starting the shaping in order to achieve this balance.

EXPERT TIP

❝ If you are crossing the cable in the same direction as the slope of your shaped edge you can continue with the cable for longer by incorporating the decrease within the crossed stitches. **❞**

BELOW Cables continued in stockinette to facilitate shaping.

Question 127:
If I discover a cable crossed in the wrong direction a few rows below, is there anything I can do about it?

First of all, look closely at your piece of knitting as a whole and decide if this mistaken cable looks glaringly obvious or if it will not be noticeable to anyone other than yourself.

If you are not happy with it you can

• remove the appropriate stitches from the needle and let them drop all the way down to the mistake.
• slip these stitches onto a double-pointed needle or cable needle, crossing them in the correct direction this time and, with a crochet hook, lift the strand above through the stitches.

• repeat these actions all the way up the column of stitches, crossing the stitches with your cable needle each time where necessary.

Another method is to cut one stitch two or three rows above the offending cable and drop these stitches to the mistake, correct it, pick them up as above, and then darn the cut ends back into the work. This method will leave you one row short, but you will have to decide whether it is more noticeable to do this or to leave the mistake!

BELOW Dropping stitches to correct cable stitch.

Question 128:
What is a mock cable?

A mock cable is a group of stitches that appear to be linked or crossed but without the use of a cable needle. There are various ways of doing this.

HOW IT'S DONE

Work a slip stitch and pass it over the other stitches after increasing to compensate for this decrease.

Row 1 Purl 3, knit 3 to last 3, purl 3.

Row 2 Knit 3, purl 3 to last 3, knit 3.

Row 3 Purl 3, slip 1, knit 2, yarn forward and on the needle to make an extra stitch, pass the slipped stitch over the two knitted stitches and the extra stitch made by working the yarn over.

Row 4 As Row 2.

Another method is to work three or four stitches, then slip them back onto the left-hand needle and take the yarn around the back of them, to the front, slip them back to the right-hand needle, and continue knitting. For a more noticeable effect, wrap the yarn several times around them. This looks attractive on stockinette or a wide rib.

The third method is to link the stitches by sewing them together after the work is finished.

LACE

Lace knitting can sometimes seem difficult, but is in fact easier to do than it looks. It is simply a combination of open increases and related decreases.

Question 129:
How do I make knitted lace?

Lace knitting is one of the most delicate and beautiful forms of knitting and looks much more complicated than it actually is. It is formed by making a series of eyelets and corresponding decreases along the row. Some patterns are formed by making eyelets on one row and decreasing on a subsequent row, but the principle of maintaining the original number of stitches remains the same.

There are simple lace patterns of only four rows and there are very complex ones such as those found in Shetland shawls where the pattern may not repeat at all but take more than 100 rows to complete!

A simple but attractive lace rib pattern of four rows worked over a multiple of six stitches is worked as follows:

ABOVE **A piece of candlelight lace.**

HOW IT'S DONE

Row 1 * Purl 2, keeping yarn at front, slip 1, knit 1, pass the slipped stitch over, knit 2 together, keeping yarn at back repeat from * to end.
Row 2 * Purl 4, knit 2, repeat from * to end.
Row 3 * Purl 2, knit 4, repeat from * to end.
Row 4 As Row 2.

The number of rows worked before repeating Row 1 can be increased to give an elongated bell shape.

Question 130:
Is there a special yarn for lace knitting?

Most lace looks best when it is worked in a plain, smooth yarn. Do not choose a yarn that is too lightly spun as this may "fluff" in the knitting and spoil the open effect. Heavily textured yarns can also hide the pattern, although lace can be effective in a fine mohair yarn worked on larger-than-normal needles. Some of the simpler patterns could also be worked in bulky yarn, and a plain white yarn of knitting worsted weight with size 6 needles is useful for your first attempts. It will be easier to see the various movements of the stitches working at this size than if you begin with a fine yarn and small needles.

Traditionally Shetland lace was, and sometimes still is, worked in cobweb one-ply. It is said that shawls made in this yarn were so fine that a whole garment could be drawn through a wedding ring. However many lace knitters work in two- or three-ply thicknesses and these are most suitable for the more complicated Shetland lace stitches.

Fine cotton and silk are also effective when knitted in lace patterns; like Shetland wool they wash and handle well and will still look good after many years of use.

BELOW Snowdrop lace socks.

Question 131:
What does "yo" mean?

"Yo" is an abbreviation for "yarn over." It is used to make an extra stitch that forms a small eyelet. It can be used before a single stitch or a decrease, but there are different actions depending on whether the preceding and following stitches are to be knitted or purled.

• After and before a knit stitch, the yarn is brought forward between the needles and passed over the right needle before the next stitch is worked.

• After a knit stitch and before a purl stitch, the yarn is brought forward, as above, then taken over the top of the needle and brought back below it (encircling the needle) before the next stitch is worked.

• After a purl stitch and before a knit stitch, the yarn is already at the front and the knit stitch is made without taking the yarn to the back, as would be the usual way.

• After a purl stitch and before another purl stitch, the yarn is taken to the back, between the needles, and brought over the top of the needle before forming the next stitch.

BELOW **Yarn brought forward before taking it around the needle for a knit stitch.**

Question 132:
What does "yrn" mean?

This abbreviation, which means "yarn round needle," is sometimes used in place of "yo," especially in British patterns. It indicates that the yarn is not in the correct place to form the next stitch but has to be taken around the needle first. It is performed differently depending on the order of stitches.

If you have just made a knit stitch and the next stitch is also knit, bring the yarn between the needles, take it around the tip of the right needle from front to back and then knit your next stitch. This makes a loop around the needle to be knitted or purled on the next row. The usual way of making this extra stitch would be to simply bring the yarn forward between the needles before making the next stitch, but there are sometimes occasions where yrn is better.

The same movements are made between a knit and a purl stitch. But if you have just made a purl stitch and your next stitch is knit, the yarn will already be at the front of your work. Take it back between the needles and bring it over the top of the right needle, all the way around and to the back again, before knitting the next stitch. For a yrn between purl and purl, take the yarn

over the top of the right needle and bring it back to the front.

Yrn is also used to indicate where two extra strands are needed on the needle in order to form a double increase. In this case the abbreviation will be "yrn twice" or "2yrn." After this increase has been made the first strand is knitted and the second is usually purled.

EXPERT TIP

66 If you are making an eyelet before a left-sloping decrease, an easy way to achieve this is to insert the needle into the next stitch as if to purl it, but instead of lifting it off, insert the needle into the following stitch as if to knit it, then lift both stitches off together. **99**

Question 133:
What is an "eyelet"?

An eyelet is a small hole produced by making a yarn over increase followed by a decrease. The techniques described on the two previous pages, moving the yarn before the next stitch, all produce eyelets. The most usual form of creating an eyelet, and one that maintains the vertical lines of stitches most closely, is to work a yarn over and then knit the next two stitches together. If the two stitches are knitted together by the slip one, knit one, pass slipped stitch over method (see page 82), the eyelet will be slightly more open but the decrease will be more noticeable.

Decreases can also be worked before eyelets and again, the method used will determine how noticeable they are and in which direction they slope.

Eyelets can be worked successively along a row, with no extra knit stitches in between, but if they are worked vertically they should have at least three rows separating them. Diagonal rows of eyelets can be worked on alternate rows as long as the knit two together method of decreasing is chosen (see page 82).

ABOVE Showing the yarn over the needle before the decrease.

LEFT Finished eyelet.

Question 134:
How do I maintain the pattern when I start shaping?

Begin with an easy four-row pattern for your first attempt. This one is a multiple of eight stitches.

HOW IT'S DONE

Row 1 Knit 3, yarn over, knit 2 together, knit 3.
Row 2 Purl.
Row 3 Knit 2, yarn over, knit 2 together, yarn over, knit 2 together, knit 2.
Row 4 Purl.

If you are now ready to repeat Row 1 and the pattern states to bind off four stitches, you will not have enough stitches to work the full pattern as the repeat is a multiple of eight and the first four of these no longer exists. There will be four stitches left for the first pattern and in this case it is best to work them in stockinette, and then begin the pattern again from the fifth stitch. When you get to the last eight stitches, work them in stockinette, too, ready to bind off four on the next row.

If you have to continue shaping by decreasing at each end of subsequent rows, you will have enough stitches in stockinette to do this four times. Maintain the next pattern for as long as possible, but when you are down to less than eight stitches each time, work in stockinette.

Where the pattern repeats over a larger number of stitches, it is sometimes possible to work a portion of the pattern, as long as increases in the pattern have a corresponding number of decreases. Once you have worked the pattern rows a number of times you will be able to see how it is shaped and where the increases and decreases are made.

Question 135:
What is the difference between lace and faggoting?

There is very little difference between lace and faggoting; both techniques result in a series of holes separated by a single strand or, at most, two strands twisted together. This is different from eyelet patterns that have at least three strands between them. For this reason lace or faggoting cannot be worked so close together in a horizontal row as eyelets since, after the first one, where the decrease is worked before the yarn over, all subsequent decreases would come after a yarn over until the last one.

Lace and faggoting are usually worked on a background of garter stitch or stockinette. Lace knitting is usually worked over alternately patterned and plain rows, while faggoting can be patterned on every row. This can cause a problem when a number of rows are worked in the same stitch, as the regular repeat of the yarn over with its corresponding decrease can cause the fabric to bias. If the yarn over comes before the decrease it will bias to the right, and if the decrease comes first it will bias to the left. Alternating these movements will prevent the bias, but the pattern will look slightly different. If the stitch is to be worked as a border, the movements can be changed halfway across a row to cancel out the bias.

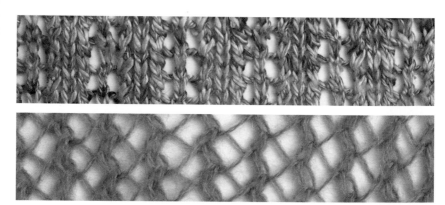

ABOVE Lace (top) and faggoting (bottom).

Question 136:
How do I follow a lace chart?

Lace charts have been in existence for some time but were not commonly used in Britain and America, where written instructions were the norm. Many knitters would have worked samples stitched into a folder, with instructions written alongside them. Being able to see the pattern would make it easier to follow.

But recently charts have become more popular, perhaps following the publication of charts for crochet, and they are much easier to follow than many lines of written instructions.

As with charts for color knitting, each square represents one stitch and a set of symbols are used to denote the stitch movements. These symbols are not always universal, but a key should be given with each chart explaining what the symbols mean. Some squares will be left blank and these should simply be knitted. Unless you are working in the round, alternate rows will be read from left to right, and as these are often plain rows this should present no problem. Along the bottom of the chart there should be a bracketing mark and possibly a description of how many stitches form one repeat of the pattern. Also, any extra stitches that form the edge of the piece should be marked, and the rows will be numbered along the side, starting at the bottom.

LEFT **Lace chart for falling leaves.**
Begin by casting on 15 stitches.

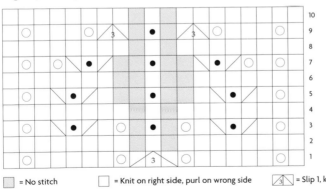

= No stitch

○ = Yarn over

• = Purl

= Knit on right side, purl on wrong side

= Knit 2 together

= Slip 1, knit 1, pass slipped stitch over

= Slip 1, knit 2 together, pass slipped stitch over

Question 137:
Why are there more squares in the chart than there are stitches?

In some lace patterns, stitches are increased in one row and decreased later. The chart must show the maximum number of stitches that are to be used in the pattern, and so the squares that have the extra stitches are usually blacked out after the decreases have been made.

They may be filled in completely or they may be crosshatched. Squares with diagonal lines indicate the slope of the decrease, and squares containing an "o" indicate an increase made by a yarn over of some kind.

There are also charts where only the patterned rows are "described" if every alternate row is knitted plain. Always read the key and the instructions for each chart carefully as different designers often have their own way of drawing charts.

Question 138:
Some patterns call for larger holes; how do I make them?

Several Shetland lace patterns, especially those for edgings, contain what are sometimes known as "grand eyelets." One of these is the "Crown of Glory" pattern. A number of decreases are worked over several rows, on the right and wrong sides of the work, before the grand eyelet is made by taking the yarn over the needle three times.

HOW IT'S DONE

Row 1 (Right side) knit 3, * slip 1, knit 1, pass slipped stitch over, knit 9, knit 2 together, knit 1, repeat from * to last 2 stitches, knit 2.

Row 2 Purl 2, * purl 1, purl 2 together, purl 7, purl 2 together through back loop, repeat from * to last 3 stitches, purl 3.

Row 3 Knit 3, * slip 1, knit 1, pass slipped stitch over, knit 2, yarn round needle 3 times, knit 3, knit 2 together, knit 1, repeat from * to last 2 stitches, knit 2.

Row 4 Purl 2, * purl 1, purl 2 together, purl 2, (knit 1, purl 1, knit 1, purl 1, knit 1) into the extra loops making 5 stitches, purl 1, purl 2 together through back, repeat from * to last 3 stitches, purl 3.

Row 5 Knit 3, * slip 1, knit 1, pass slipped stitch over, knit 6, knit 2 together, knit 1, repeat from * to last 2 stitches, knit 2.

Row 6 Purl 2, * purl 1, purl 2 together, purl 6, repeat from * ending last repeat purl 3.

Row 7 Knit 3, * knit 1, (yarn over, knit 1) 6 times, knit 1, repeat from * to last 2 stitches, knit 2.

Row 8 Purl to end.

Rows 9 and 10 Knit to end.

Row 11 Purl to end.

Row 12 Knit to end.

RIGHT Fine yarns have been used to great effect for this Shetland lace top and scarf.

Question 139:
What is the traditional method of creating a Shetland shawl?

There are two ways of constructing a Shetland shawl.

Begin with a narrow edging, knitted lengthways, slightly longer than the finished measurement to accommodate the corners. Next pick up one-quarter of the stitches from the straight side of the edging and knit a wide border with decreases at each end of alternate rows to form the corners; leave these stitches on a spare needle or a length of yarn and repeat the process for each of the next three borders. Return to the stitches left from the first border and, using them as the first row, knit a center, taking one of the stitches from each side border and knitting it together with the last stitch of the center on every alternate row. Graft the last row of the center to the stitches of the fourth border. Finally, join the shaped edges of the wide border and the cast-on, bound-off edges of the edging with a loose over-sewing or herringbone stitch.

As can be seen, this method requires some sewing and grafting of the pieces. Its wide border could be knitted in one piece using circular needles with corner stitches marked to show where the decreases should be made.

The second method uses double-pointed or circular needles, which leaves very little sewing or grafting to be done.

Using an invisible, or knitted cast-on, make the center first on straight needles; when it is the required size, change to circular needles and knit across the last row of stitches, increase one stitch at the corner, and mark it. Pick up the same number of stitches down the side of the center square, increase at the corner and mark it again. Repeat this for the other two sides of the square, increase and mark the last stitch. It is useful to mark this stitch with a different color to denote the beginning of the round. When all the stitches are joined, work in rounds, increasing at each side of the marked stitches on alternate rows by working a yarn over. When the border is finished, do not cast off the stitches but cast on a few extra at the beginning of the round with a pair of straight needles and knit the narrow edging, again, picking up and knitting a stitch from the border, together with the last stitch of each alternate row of the edging until you are a few rows short of a corner; work a few rows of edging here without taking up one of the border stitches to give some extra fullness. Finally join the cast-on and cast-off rows of the edging together.

This second method can also be constructed from a diagonal center by casting on one stitch, increasing at the beginning of every row to the halfway point, then decreasing at the beginning of every row until one stitch remains.

Remember when using circular needles to produce garter stitch that alternate rows must be purled.

BELOW Shetland shawl constructed using the first method described in the text.

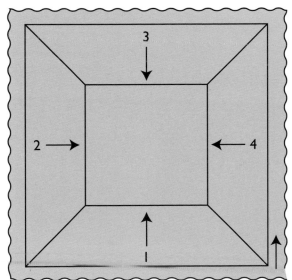

Start here and work edging first in direction of arrow.

Pick up stitches from straight side of edging and work inner border, decreasing at each corner. Or work four borders separately and join with flat seams. Finally, work center square, knitting side stitches together with corresponding stitch of borders two and four. Graft last row to border three.

Question 140:
How do I create a pointed edging for a shawl?

Shaped edgings are made by increasing stitches for a number of rows and then decreasing them over the next few rows, either by working two together or binding them off.

One of the traditional Shetland edgings forms a series of small, pointed diamonds on a garter stitch background and is worked as shown below.

For a pennant-type edging, using bind-offs instead of decreasing, work as shown until the edging is as deep as you want, then bind off the extra stitches that were made by the yarn overs.

LEFT Shetland shawl with deep scalloped edging.

Question 141:
What is "filet" lace?

Filet lace is also formed from yarn overs but unlike other types of lace, which is soft and rounded, filet lace is based on squares. It is usually worked in cotton for a firm fabric and bears a close resemblance to filet crochet.

Filet lace is sometimes given in chart form, in which case each square represents three stitches not one, as is usually the case.

HOW IT'S DONE

Each space takes four rows to complete.

Row 1 Knit 4, yarn over twice, slip the next 2 stitches knitwise and pass the first over the second, slip the next stitch and pass the second over it, return this stitch to the left-hand needle and knit it, knit 4.
Row 2 Knit 4, knit 1, purl 1, knit 1.
Row 3 As Row 1.
Row 4 As Row 2.

This completes one block and space, divided by twisted strands across the center.

10 OTHER DECORATIVE EFFECTS

Here we look at some of the many different ways of embellishing knitting, either during the work or after the main piece is finished, to make it even more special.

Question 142:
How do I make bobbles?

Bobbles can be made in any size, but the method of working is more or less the same in each case:

Work to the position you want the bobble, and increase in the next stitch by working knit and purl alternately, or by working knit, yarn over alternately. You now have several new stitches on the right-hand needle. Turn the work so that the wrong side is facing and purl these stitches, turn again, and knit them. Repeat these two rows again for a fairly large bobble—even more times if you want a really large one and have increased more stitches. When the bobble is the size you want, decrease the stitches back to one again.

Bobbles do not have to be worked in the same fabric or even the same color as the background. If you want to work them in contrast yarn, use a separate piece for each bobble and darn the ends firmly into the back of it afterward.

You can also work bobbles using a crochet hook after the work is finished. This is a useful method if you want to make different colored bobbles.

Work four or five single crochet into one stitch, work one more row of single crochet, then work one double crochet into each stitch, leaving the last loop of each on the hook. Draw the yarn through all the loops and fasten off. Darn the tail end over the stitch above and back into the bobble.

Question 143:
What is the difference between a knot and a bobble?

Knots are much smaller than bobbles and are worked over one or two rows without turning the work.

There are several ways to do this.

- Knit 1, purl 1, knit 1 all into the same stitch; on the next row knit or purl 3 together.
- Knit 1, purl 1, knit 1 into same stitch, pass the first and second stitches over the third.
- Knit 1 and cast on a few stitches, then either cast them off again or knit them all together.

Unlike bobbles, knots do not stand out very well from the background fabric unless they are worked *en bloc* or as an all-over pattern.

Question 144:
How do I decrease several stitches at once?

If you have increased several times to make a fairly large bobble it can be difficult to decrease back to one stitch on one row. One method is to pass the stitches, one at a time, over the stitch nearest to the point of the right-hand needle. This can make the bobble turn slightly toward the left.

Another method is to decrease gradually over a number of rows; instead of working straight on the increased stitches, decrease one at the beginning and end of each row, or work three together in the center. The last three stitches are easier to work together if they are purled. Bobbles decreased in this way will not be as round as those where all the stitches are decreased at once.

A third method is to work the last row with a similar-sized crochet hook, pulling the strand through the stitches all together.

Question 145:
How do I make leaf shapes?

Leaves and flower shapes are started in a similar way to bobbles, by increasing several stitches in one. They can be combined with cables and bobbles to form really attractive and intricate-looking designs, and they are not difficult to make. They look best worked on a background of reverse stockinette where they will stand out well.

There are different methods of shaping them after the increases.

- Increase several stitches, then work the knit and purl stitches as set for a few rows. Decrease three stitches together at the center of the leaf on alternate rows until there is one stitch left. Work this stitch as a purl stitch after the leaf is completed.
- Work to the point the leaf is to be made, then work a yarn over before and after the next stitch. Continue to work yarn overs at each side of this stitch on alternate rows until the leaf is the size you want. Work paired decreases at each edge of the leaf on the following alternate rows. Complete as above.
- To work pairs of leaves: work to the point required and make three stitches out of one. On the

following alternate row work to one stitch before the increase, knit two together, yarn over, knit one, yarn over, knit two together through back loop; work one row as set; work next row as above but purl the stitches that were the yarn overs of the previous row. Continue increasing in this way and working the extra stitches in purl until the leaves are the required size. Place a small bobble at the top of the knit stitch, or work a few eyelets to look like a flower.

ABOVE Leaves made using the second method described in the text.

Question 146:
How do I knit an entrelac pattern?

Entrelac is worked by using short row shaping, in other words, working over a few stitches, turning and working back, and then working over one or two more stitches on subsequent rows.

1 The full count of stitches is cast on to begin with; on the following row only two stitches are purled, turned, then knitted. On the next two rows three stitches are worked, then four stitches, five stitches, and so on, until you have a triangle. At this point the work is not turned ready to purl, but two more stitches are taken from the cast-on row and the procedure is repeated. Continue like this until you have a row of triangles, joined together by their points.

2 It is easier to see what you are doing if you now join in a second color for the row of blocks. Pick up and knit one stitch for each row from the first triangle. Turn and purl back, but when you get to the end of the row, work the last stitch together with one from the next triangle. Continue taking up one stitch each time until all the stitches have been used up.

Rejoin your first color and work the second row of blocks in the same way. If you want your piece to have straight sides you will need to work triangles at the edges by decreasing on alternate rows.

Question 147:
How do I trim an edge with crochet?

It is useful to know how to do a few simple crochet stitches to use with knitting. A crochet hook can also be a helpful tool for picking up stitches and for casting on and off, as well as for button loops and more decorative trims.

To work a crochet edge on a finished piece of knitting, either along the cast-on or bound-off edge, or along the side edges, use a hook the same size, or one size smaller, than your knitting needles, join the yarn to the first stitch at the edge, then insert the hook under two strands; bring the yarn over the hook from the back to the front, and pull it

through the edge stitch with the hook; * insert the hook under the next two strands and do the same so that there are two stitches on the hook; bring the yarn from the back to the front and pull it through these two stitches to make one. This is one single crochet. Repeat from * until you have worked all the stitches along the edge and there is one loop on the crochet hook. If you have to work around a corner make three single crochet into the corner stitch.

After you have set up this foundation row there are many books containing crochet patterns that you can follow for a decorative edging.

BELOW **Both the top and right-hand edges have been trimmed with crochet.**

RIGHT The star-shaped buttons complement the star pattern used on this cardigan.

Other Decorative Effects

Question 148:
How do I add fringe?

If you want to add fringe after all the knitting is completed, you'll need a crochet hook.

Cut three or four lengths of yarn a little over twice as long as the finished fringe. Fold these strands in half. Insert the crochet hook through one stitch at the edge of the knitting and place the folded end of the strands in the hook, draw it through the stitch, and then pass the cut ends through this loop. Pull on the cut ends to draw it up firmly, then trim the fringe to an equal length when completed.

Long fringe can also be tied together, with half the strands from one "tassel" tied to half of those from its neighboring one. If this is repeated at staggered intervals it will produce a diamond effect.

Fringe can also be made from the knitting itself, but only along a side edge. At the end of the bind-off row leave a few stitches and let them unravel to the cast-on row. Or cast on several stitches and knit for the required length, then cast off some of them and unravel

as above. This knitted fringing can have its edge stitches knitted in a pattern. Cables, or twisted stitches, will resemble braid, or you can use eyelets for a more delicate fringe.

EXPERT TIP

66 Readymade fringing can be bought from fabric stores. Buy more than you need and separate some threads from a surplus piece. Use these to add embroidery stitches to your knitting. This way the fringe will not look isolated from the rest of the piece. 99

Question 149:
How do I make a loop stitch?

Loops are made by wrapping the yarn a number of times around the thumb or fingers, depending on the method used, and then anchoring it with a knit stitch. Make sure that you work a gauge swatch first, as loop stitches are much looser than those made in the normal way.

Cast on the required number of stitches and work two rows of stockinette or garter stitch.

Knit one, knit the second stitch but leave it on the needle, bring the yarn forward and take it under the left thumb and back up between the needles to the back, knit the stitch again and slip it off the needle but keep the loop on the thumb. Insert the left needle back through the two stitches just made and knit them together. Slip the thumb out of the loop. Knit one or more stitches, then repeat the steps for the next loop.

These loops are firmly anchored and can be cut afterward to give a soft pile.

In the second method the loops are made on the wrong side rows by taking the yarn over the fingers of the left hand; it is usually worked on garter stitch. Knit one, insert the needle into the next stitch, and bring the yarn over the right needle then back and around the middle finger of the left hand as many times as you want. Slip this group of strands back onto the left-hand needle and knit them. To make them slightly more secure, knit into the back and front of the loops at stage two, then slip the first stitch made over the second. These loops are not anchored as fast as those in the first method, so do not cut them.

Question 150:
How do I knit with beads?

Before you begin your knitting the beads need to be threaded onto the yarn—in reverse order if you are working with different colors. Unless you are working with a great number, or very heavy beads, thread them all at once. Thread a needle that will easily pass through the eye of the bead with doubled sewing cotton so that there are cut ends at one side and a loop at the other. Pass the yarn through this loop and fold it back. Pick up the beads with the needle point and slide them down the shaft and onto the yarn.

If you just knit to the point where the bead is to be placed and then knit it in the normal way it will appear on the wrong side of the work! This is fine if you are working in garter stitch with no distinguishable right and wrong side. If you have already set the position of the right side then work purl garter stitch instead.

To place the bead so that it will appear on the right side of stockinette, purl the stitch before and after the bead. Insert the needle into the back of the stitch, push the bead close up to the left needle, take the yarn around the needle in the normal way, taking the bead with it, knit the stitch and push the

bead through to the right side.

A second method is to knit to the position of the bead, bring the yarn forward, position the bead, slip the stitch purlwise, take the yarn back and knit the next stitch.

Beads can also be added if you use a crochet hook fine enough to go through the eye of the bead, and then knit the "beaded" stitch with the hook.

ABOVE Shrug cardigan knitted with beads.

Question 151:
What is I-cord and how do I make it?

The term I-cord was coined by Elizabeth Zimmerman as an abbreviation for "Idiot's Delight." It is a simple method of making a cord of varying thickness and is easily adaptable for alternative stitches or multicolors. Its appearance is the same as that produced by a French knitter, or knitting bobbin—a wooden spool with nails at the top. There are also mechanical versions of these bobbins, known as knitting mills.

I-cord is made using two double-pointed needles.

Cast on a few stitches, no more than six, and knit one row. Push the stitches to the other end of the needle and knit them again. Repeat this action, pulling the yarn tightly before beginning each successive row. When the cord is long enough knit all the stitches together. Alternatively, if you have six stitches, knit three together twice and then knit two together on the following row.

Another way of making a knitted cord is to cast on a length of stitches and then to bind them off again on the next row. Any of the cast-on and bind-off methods can be used. For a wider version of this cord, work a few rows of stockinette before binding off; the knitting will naturally roll back on itself with the reverse side showing.

Question 152:
How do I embroider knitting?

There are a number of ways of embellishing knitting with embroidery. Because the knitted stitches form a grid pattern it can be used to work cross stitch. Use a rounded point or tapestry needle and insert it between the stitches so that the yarn is not split. Take care not to pull the embroidery yarn too tightly or the knitting will lose some of its elasticity.

You can also work chain stitch in any direction on knitting just as on fabric, but for a quick method use a crochet hook to form the chains. Hold the yarn at the back of the fabric, insert the crochet hook through the stitch, catch the embroidery yarn, and pull it through; insert the hook through the next stitch and repeat the action. Continue in this way as required.

Blanket stitch looks effective along the edge, but can also be used elsewhere in the piece, as can other, loosely worked embroidery stitches such as stem stitch and lazy daisy. French knots, eyelets, as in broderie anglaise, and bullion knots can all be used effectively, and appliques, either readymade, or knitted to shape, can be applied with hem stitch or blanket stitch.

Question 153:
How do I make flaps?

Pieces of knitting can be made separately and then knitted into the main piece, at random or regularly spaced as you wish. The pieces to make the flaps are best knitted in garter stitch, or moss stitch if you want them to lie flat. They can be made in the same yarn or a contrasting one, and could be knitted onto a striped row made in the same contrasting color.

Knit the pieces first, of any size and shape, and leave the last row of each on the needle. When you come to the position you want to place them on the knitting, position the needle with the flap in front of the next stitches on the body and knit the stitches of the flap together with their equivalent stitches from the main piece.

You could also add small lengths of I-cord, spirals, and so on, in a similar way.

Question 154:
How do I make tucks?

Tucks are like hems that appear within the main fabric of the piece rather than at the edge. They are best worked in fine yarn, as there will be three thickness of fabric at that point. The yarn for the tuck does not necessarily need to be the same yarn as you are using to knit the rest of the piece.

To make a tuck, work a number of rows and then work one row on a size larger needle, or one row in reverse stockinette, so that the ridge row is on the right side. This row will be the fold line. Work the same number of rows for the second half of the tuck. If you finish at the end of a purl row, work as follows: * take one stitch from the needle and one ridge from the first row of the tuck and knit them together, knit the next stitch from the needle; repeat from * to end. If you finish at the end of a knit row, purl the stitches together.

Tucks can also be made with picot edges, just as in making a hem, or decorated with knots or bobbles, made in a different stitch or worked in a different yarn.

BELOW A sample showing a picot edge tuck (top) and a plain edge tuck (bottom).

Picot edge

Plain edge

Question 155:
What is ruched knitting?

Ruching is made by increasing across the row, working a few rows, and then decreasing again. It can be used as an all-over pattern, but remember to base the measurements of your gauge swatch on the decreased portion of the stitch.

It is often worked with different-sized needles, or different yarns, as well as having extra stitches. For example:

- Cast on any number of stitches and knit seven rows.

- Change to two sizes larger needles and increase in every stitch.
- Work several rows in stockinette, or a pattern of your choice.
- Decrease in every stitch.
- Change back to the smaller needles and knit seven rows.

Any number of rows can be worked on any number of stitches. Bands of stockinette could be worked without the increasings in some places.

Question 156:
How do I make a fluted edge?

A fluted edge or frill can be knitted either from the beginning or after the work is finished.

To knit it from the beginning, cast on four times as many stitches as you require for the width of the body. Work a few rows of garter or moss stitch so that the edge will not curl up. Knit one or two rows of stockinette then decrease in every stitch on the next row. Work one or two more rows of stockinette and decrease again as before. This is just an example; these figures can be altered to give a wider or deeper frill.

A fluted edge can also be worked in a stitch resembling small bells, which is described on the right.

To work a fluted edge from the top down after the work is completed, pick up and knit one stitch for each stitch along the cast-on edge. Purl one row. On the next row work twice into every stitch. Repeat these two rows, or work more plain rows between the increase row, until the frill is as full and as long as you want. Bind off in the usual way or use a picot edge bind-off, or add beads to the bind-off row.

HOW IT'S DONE

Cast on a multiple of 11 stitches + 4.

Row 1 Purl 4, knit 7 to end, purl 4.
Row 2 Knit 4, purl 7 to end, knit 4.
Row 3 As Row 1.
Row 4 As Row 2.
Row 5 * Purl 4, slip 1, knit 1, pass slipped stitch over, knit 3, knit 2 together; repeat from * to end, purl 4.
Row 6 Work stitches as set.
Row 7 * Purl 4, slip 1, knit 1, pass slipped stitch over, knit 1, knit 2 together, purl 4, repeat from * to end.
Row 8 Work stitches as set.
Row 9 * Purl 4, slip 2 together knitwise, knit 1, pass slipped stitches over, repeat from * to end, purl 4.
Row 10 Either continue in wide rib as set or work in reverse stockinette until you are ready to start the main part of the work.

Question 157:
How do I make knitted spirals?

There are three methods of making spirals. In the horizontal method you may need to work a test one first, because once you have started the spiral its length cannot be altered. You can make them separately and stitch them on or work them along a bind-off row.

To make separate spirals, cast on a number of stitches, then work twice into each stitch on the next row(s). Bind off loosely. To work them along a bind-off edge, bind off a number of stitches, cast on using the loop method, then immediately bind them off again, bind off a few more stitches, and repeat the cast-on bind-off.

HOW IT'S DONE

To make a spiral that can be altered in length work it vertically:

Row 1 Cast on 8 stitches, knit 2 together each stitch, cast on 8.
Row 2 Knit 8, knit 3 together, knit 2 together.
Row 3 Knit 2 together each stitch, cast on 8.
Row 4 Repeat rows 2 and 3 until the spiral is as long as you want.

BELOW Horizontal spirals worked along the bound-off edge.

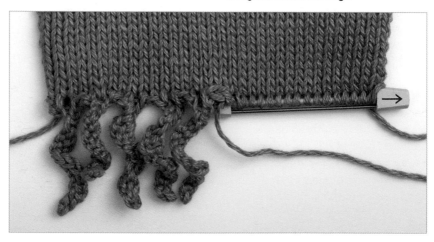

Question 158:
What is the best way to insert a pocket?

The simplest way is to sew on a patch pocket. Knit a piece the size and shape that you want, finish it with a border that won't become loose and baggy, and stitch it to the finished garment. Use a similar method to Swiss darning, working through both thicknesses, for a neat finish.

An inset pocket is worked as the garment is knitted. The inside of the pocket is worked first and the stitches left on a holder. The body is then knitted to the position of the top of the pocket, and the stitches that will form the border are placed on a holder while the stitches from the pocket back are knitted across to replace them. The stitches from the holder are picked up and worked into a border later, and the inside of the pocket is stitched down after the piece is finished.

There is also a way of making the pocket back all in one with the main piece. Knit to the position of the pocket, then turn and work on these stitches only for twice the depth of the pocket. Leave the stitches on each side of it on stitch holders while you work. When the pocket is the required length, knit the next row and knit across all of the stitches from the following stitch holder; turn and purl all of the stitches, including those from the second holder. When the work is finished stitch the sides of the pocket together. A border is optional for this pocket, but a row of single crochet would strengthen the edge.

Pockets can also be inserted in the side seams by picking up stitches from the side edges of the back and knitting flaps, which will be stitched to the inside of the fronts when the work is made up. Work a row of single crochet along the front edge to neaten it.

EXPERT TIP

66 You can also add a pocket as an afterthought. Cut a stitch at the center of what would be the top row of the pocket. Pull out the length of yarn for the required width and place the live stitches on two separate stitch holders. Work the pocket lining downward from the top holder, and work the border up from the lower holder. 99

Question 159:
What other embellishments are there?

There are not many edgings that are hardwearing enough to be used at the cuffs and hems of garments. However, many more delicate pieces can be decorated with lacy edges, either knitted on, as for a Shetland shawl, or stitched on when completed.

This one is knitted on:

HOW IT'S DONE

Bind on 25 stitches.

Row 1 Knit to last stitch and knit this together with the corresponding stitch of the cast-on edge.
Row 2 Slip 1, knit to end.
Row 3 As Row 1.
Row 4 Slip 1, knit 3 (yarn over, knit 2 together) to last stitch, knit 1.
Row 5 As Row 1.
Row 6 Slip 1, knit 4 (yarn over, knit 2 together) to last 2 stitches, knit 2.
Row 7 As Row 1.
Row 8 Slip 1, knit 5 (yarn over, knit 2 together) to last 2 stitches, knit 2.

Row 9 Bind off 3 and complete as Row 1.
Row 10 As Row 2.
Row 11 As Row 1.
Row 12 Knit to end and increase in last stitch.
Repeat the pattern from Row 3.

Knitted flowers, buttons, or beads can be stitched on, or lower edges of garments can be decorated with knitted pom poms, balls, or bell shapes.

To make a bell, cast on a number of stitches, approximately 12, and work a picot hem (see page 39). Knit two together across the next row. Purl two together on the next row and fasten off, leaving a long tail to sew the side seam and darn it back in to be used to sew the bell to the edge of the garment.

Question 160:
What is duplicate stitch?

Duplicate stitch, also called Swiss darning, was first introduced as a method of reinforcing the heels and toes of socks, and was worked over the tops of stitches that had worn thin, hence the name.

Duplicate stitch is more often used now as a means of working some stitches in a different color after a piece is finished; especially the small patches of color sometimes required in a Jacquard pattern, when it would be untidy to knit in one or two stitches with a separate length of yarn.

To work duplicate stitch, thread the required color of yarn into a blunt-ended needle and, working from right to left, mimic the shape of the knitted stitch by bringing the needle up through the center, from right to left around the back of the stitch, out at the top, and back down through the center again. Move along to the next stitch and repeat the action. Work the next row from left to right or turn the work upside down if it is easier. If you are working a vertical line, start at the bottom and work upward.

PICKING UP AND JOINING

Sewing or making up—in other words, assembling the pieces after the knitting is finished—can make or mar a garment. Here we look at how to join pieces successfully.

Question 161:
How do I pick up stitches along a straight edge?

Picking up and knitting stitches, or knitting up, is a technique that can often spoil the finished appearance of an item. The stitches should be picked up consistently along the edge, either through a whole stitch or half a stitch, and they should be spaced evenly. Use a needle one or two sizes smaller than that used for the main piece.

To pick up along a cast on or bound-off edge, pick up stitch for stitch and decrease on the first row if necessary. Insert the needle under both loops of the first stitch, wrap the yarn around the needle in the same way as for a knit stitch, and draw it through. Repeat this action along the row until you have the required number of stitches. Remember that the first row you work will be a wrong side row.

To pick up stitches evenly from a side edge, unless the pattern states otherwise, you will find that three stitches to every four rows usually works out neatly. Insert the needle between the first and second stitches and draw the loop through as above. There should be a chain edge lying behind the needle if you have worked in stockinette. If you are using a very bulky yarn, insert the needle through the center of the first stitch, so that there is half a stitch lying behind the needle at the end.

BELOW **Picking up stitches one stitch in.**

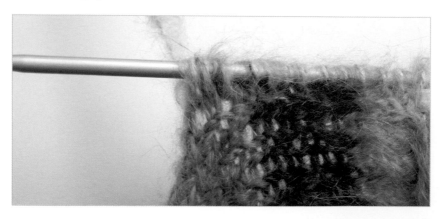

Question 162:
How do I pick up stitches around a curved edge?

The most likely place where this will be necessary is around a neck edge, and as this is a very noticeable point on a garment it needs to be done neatly.

The first section of stitches of a round neck will either have been bound off or left on a holder. It is a simple matter to knit these up, although they will look slightly different from the rest of the knitted up stitches if they have not been bound off first, as there will be no layer of stitches behind them. The next section will be the curve where the stitches should be picked up under two strands. If the shaping has been worked one or two stitches in from the edge, do not pick up from these stitches or you will spoil the line; if possible, work within the shapings to keep the curve as smooth as possible. The third part is the vertical section where the stitches should be picked up from between the first and second stitch as above and worked into approximately three out of four rows. Stitches picked up from a curved edge need to be worked in rib, or decreases will need to be made to maintain the shape of the curve.

It is also possible to pick up stitches from straight and curved edges with a crochet hook, working a single crochet into each stitch. This can be made to look more obviously decorative if the hook is inserted well inside the edges to form a long stitch.

EXPERT TIP

66 Use a circular needle to pick up the stitches, and then simply leave the work on it for a short while. It will then be easier to see if you have too few, or too many, stitches than if the work were distorted on a straight needle. 99

Question 163:
How do I know how many stitches to pick up?

If you want to be really accurate rather than relying on the three stitches for every four rows, then you will need to take note of how many stitches and rows you had to 1 inch (2.5 cm) in your gauge swatch.

For example, if you have seven stitches to 1 inch (2.5 cm) and ten rows to 1 inch (2.5 cm) divide the stitches, seven, by the rows, ten, which equals 0.7, and multiply this by 12 to see how many stitches you need to pick up in every 12 rows. The result is 8.4 stitches, which you can round down to eight. Eight stitches for every 12 rows are the same as two stitches for every three rows, so that is how many to pick up.

Obviously these figures will vary depending on the gauge you obtain for your own knitting, but the method will be the same. I used the number 12 at random as it was a simple multiplier and seemed a reasonable number of rows. You could just as easily use any number to suit yourself.

Question 164:
How do I make buttonholes?

There are buttonholes made over two or more stitches and there are single-hole buttonholes.

RIGHT
Horizontal one-row buttonhole (top); horizontal two-row buttonhole (bottom).

Single-hole buttonhole
The single-hole buttonholes are usually made on small items such as baby garments. They are simple eyelets made by working a yarn over, knit two together. A bigger hole can be made by wrapping the yarn over twice and dropping the extra loop on the return row. Place the yarn over two or three stitches in from the edge so that it is not pulled too much. This actually applies to all buttonholes.

Horizontal buttonhole

A basic horizontal buttonhole is made by binding off the required number of stitches on the right side row and casting them on again on the return row. It is slightly neater if the first cast-on stitch is worked as an increase in the last stitch before casting on the others plus one, which is knitted together with the next stitch.

A one-row horizontal buttonhole is worked as follows: slip one purlwise, take yarn back, slip next stitch purlwise and pass first stitch over it; repeat for as many stitches as you need to cast off. Slip the last stitch back onto the left needle and turn. With yarn at the back, cast-on (using the cable method) all the buttonhole stitches plus one extra, bringing the yarn forward before placing this last one on the left needle. Turn and slip one stitch knitwise, then pass the extra stitch over it.

All buttonholes look better and are stronger if they are neatened after the work is finished.

Question 165:
What is "blocking"?

Blocking means to "set" the stitches and pieces in the shape that they are meant to retain. It is usually done immediately after all the pieces of knitting have been finished, but it can sometimes be used as a remedial measure for something that has lost its shape, or needs a little stretching. However, do read the ball band of the yarn first to make sure that this process is suitable. Anything knitted in intarsia or Jacquard will be improved enormously by blocking, as will items made in stockinette, but take care with more textured stitches such as Aran patterns or ribs, as these can be spoiled by being flattened!

Before you begin to join seams, lay the pieces out flat, make sure that they are the correct measurements, and pin them into place on a board or thick towel. Then, either spray them with a fine mist of cool water and leave them to dry naturally, away from direct heat or sunlight, or gently steam press them by hovering the iron just above the pieces. Never slide the iron across the work or press down on it. (The exception to this is knitted cotton lace, which can be pressed quite flat.) When you have finished blocking and pressing, leave the items in place for a few moments and then join the seams. They will have lost some of their tendency to curl, and stitching should be much easier.

Question 166:
How do I make vertical buttonholes?

Vertical buttonholes are made by leaving some stitches unworked while completing a few rows on another group of stitches. When the buttonhole is long enough, usually only four or five rows, break off the yarn, return to the stitches that are left on the holder, and knit them for the same number of rows. Work across all the stitches and continue to the next buttonhole.

Vertical buttonholes are best worked in any place where there is a downward pull. If they are worked at the front edges of a cardigan they will pull open sideways. Horizontal buttonholes are best here where the stress will pull the buttonhole tighter around the button.

ABOVE **The left-hand side is the first side of the buttonhole completed.**

Question 167:
How do I work out the positioning of buttonholes?

Whichever direction you are working the bands, work the button band first and then make sure that you work the buttonhole band with the same number of stitches and rows.

On a vertical band, mark with dressmaker's pins where you want your top and bottom buttons to be positioned. Fold the work in half so that the two pins meet, and place another pin at the halfway point. Space other pins evenly between these to mark the position of your buttonholes. Count the rows between the pins to be accurate.

On a horizontal band, note how many stitches you used in the button band and pick up and knit the same number for your buttonhole band. You can either space the buttonholes by using pins and counting stitches as for vertical bands, or you can calculate the spacing more accurately using math. When you cast off the stitches for your buttonhole, remember to count the stitch that is left on the needle as the first stitch of your next sequence.

The spaces between the buttonholes will number one less than the buttonholes themselves. Six buttonholes will have five spaces between them; don't count the top and bottom stitches for now. Assuming you have 72 stitches on the needles and want to make five buttonholes of two stitches each, that will take up ten stitches. Take away these ten from the 72, leaving 62. You now need four spaces within those 62 stitches, but need to leave some stitches at the top and bottom of the band, so make a guess and take away six—three for the top and three for the bottom. That leaves you with 56. Fifty-six divided by four equals 14; so you need 14 stitches between buttonholes and three at the top and bottom.

Question 168:
How do I sew in a sleeve with a shaped top?

A sleeve with a rounded top is often joined to the body after the shoulder and side seams have been joined and after the underarm seam of the sleeve has been joined. It needs to be turned right side out and inserted into the shaped armhole with the sleeve seam matching the side seam, and the head of the sleeve at the shoulder seam. Pin these two points and then pin the sleeve around the armhole at intervals of 1 or 2 inches (2.5–5 cm). Gather in any fullness in the sleeve between the pins as you go. If you find that the armhole is larger than the sleeve, then you will need to undo the sleeve head and reknit a few more rows. When the sleeve is pinned in place, attach it to the body with a backstitch seam worked as close to the edge as possible so that it is not too bulky.

This is the correct method for setting in a sleeve, but I find that it is just as neat and easier to work if the sleeve is attached to the body before the side and sleeve seams are joined. Similarly for a raglan sleeve, join the sloped edges first and then join the side and sleeve seams all in one.

Question 169:
What is the best method of joining pieces of knitting?

This depends on which seams you are joining and also what stitch you have used at the edge.

For side edges, mattress stitch or invisible seaming is the neatest and most unobtrusive. Use the same yarn you used for the knitting, or a closely matching yarn if you have knitted in something very bulky. Thread the yarn into a blunt-ended needle with a large enough eye and attach it firmly to the bottom edge of one side seam. With right sides uppermost and the seams side by side, take one stitch from each side seam, half or one stitch in from the edge. Pull the yarn so that the edges are drawn together. Shoulder seams and other bound-off edges can also be joined in this way, working one stitch in from the binding off.

For loose edges, such as those on lace knitting, use an oversewing seam; place the right sides of the work together and bring the needle up through both pieces, over the seam and up through the stitch of the row above. This seam can also be worked on the right sides with a contrasting yarn to give a decorative finish.

If you are joining edges worked in different directions, consider knitting them on as you go rather than sewing them on later. Or work a row of double crochet along the bottom edge and attach the edging to it with a running stitch or backstitch.

Question 170:
What is "grafting"?

Grafting is sometimes known as Kitchener stitch (no one seems to know why) and is a means of joining two pieces of knitting by imitating the stitches. The easiest stitch to graft is stockinette, as the method of joining these pieces is similar to duplicate stitch. The stitches should be left on the needles while they are about to be grafted, but it is easier to see how it works if they are taken off the needles. Lay the two pieces to be joined with the open stitches facing each other and with the right sides uppermost. Thread the same yarn used for the knitting into a blunt-ended sewing needle and attach it to the first stitch on the right edge of the lower piece.

Bring the needle out from back to front through the center of the stitch and take it behind and up through the corresponding stitch on the top piece; bring it down and back into the center of the first stitch, along the back of it and out up through the center of the second stitch. Continue in this way along the row, taking one stitch from each edge until they are all attached. Keep the size of the stitches the same as those of your knitted pieces.

Garter stitch can also be grafted this way and is easiest to work if one side has ended on a wrong side row and the other on a right side. Your grafting thread should form a line of ridges along the right side row.

Question 171:
How do I graft ribbed pieces together?

There are two ways of doing this:

•   Work the stitches as they come, remembering that if the rib lies in opposite directions, such as at shoulder seams, it will be half a stitch out. Bring the needle up through the first knit stitch on the lower piece. Now take it down through the first stitch on the upper piece, then along to the side of the purl stitch and up through it. Now take it down through the first knit stitch on the lower piece, then across and down through the purl stitch. Now go up through the same part of the purl stitch on the upper piece, across the front of it and down through the other side. Finally, go through the center of the lower purl stitch, then across and up through the next knit stitch.

•   Work all the knit then all the purl stitches. Graft each knit stitch together as for stockinette, then turn the work over so that the other side is facing. The purl stitches will now appear as knit, and can be grafted in the same way.

Question 172:
How do I attach zippers and buttons?

Before you start your knitting, decide where zippers and buttons are to be placed. Work a few stitches in garter stitch at the side edges where you wish to insert a zipper. This will help the work to lie flat. If you forget, or the zipper is an afterthought, work a row of crochet stitches along the edges. Because knitting is elastic and zippers are not, it is sometimes difficult to attach them to the work neatly, especially on the wrong side. This can be Improved a little by covering the wrong side of the knitting with some bias tape or by working some extra stitches along one side edge to form a flap that will cover the zipper when it is fastened.

Attach the zipper before joining all the pieces of knitting, and if the garment has a conspicuous pattern or stripes, make sure that they match each other correctly. Tack it to the knitting, being careful not to stretch it, and then with the zipper opened, backstitch it close to the teeth with sewing thread in a color matching the yarn as closely as possible. Finally slip stitch over the edge of the zipper so that it does not curl back.

It is easier to buy buttons first and then make the buttonholes to fit them, rather than the other way around. Try to match them to the yarn, in other words, use a good-quality button on an expensive yarn and a large button on a bulky yarn. Shank buttons are usually better suited to thick yarns so that the buttonhole band can sit neatly beneath them when done up. If you cannot find suitable buttons then you can make them.

Attach the buttons with the yarn you used for knitting, or if it is too thick to go through the holes, split it and twist it slightly after attaching it to the fabric to avoid it separating. If you think that the button may disappear through loosely knitted stitches, attach a smaller button or a piece of non-fraying fabric to the back as you sew.

EXPERT TIP

66 Buy an extra button, and thread some of your yarn through it. Pin or tape this to your pattern or notebook and you will always have spares for repairs. 99

Question 173:
What method should I use to create an elasticized waistband?

Again, this is something that should be planned for before beginning the knitting, as there is more than one method.

The simplest way is to create a row of eyelets two or three rows before the bind-off row, and then thread this with a narrow piece of elastic or with a knitted or twisted cord.

A second method, where the work looks as neat on the wrong side as it does on the right, is to create a casing for the elastic by knitting a hem. Work a reverse row at the fold line to help the hem to lie flat and use elastic as deep as the hem, otherwise it will twist inside the casing. Leave a gap at the inside of one of the side seams and thread the elastic through with a large safety pin.

The least bulky method, and one that can be used as an afterthought, is to stitch the elastic to the inside of the border with large herringbone stitches. Use the knitting yarn if it is not too thick, and fasten it to the top edge of the knitting. Take the needle diagonally across the elastic, and then under the next stitch from right to left. Bring it up diagonally

and under the next stitch at the top from right to left. Continue in this way to the end of the work, and then fasten off and join the two edges of the elastic together to fit.

There is one final method of attaching elastic that is useful at the hem edge of cotton garments that have become too loose. Thread shirring elastic through the backs of the knit stitches on the wrong side of the rib several rows apart. This will help for a while, but shirring elastic is not very strong and it is only a temporary measure.

BELOW Herringbone stitch.

12 HINTS AND TIPS

Some special "tricks of the trade" can help correct mistakes. Others, such as adapting patterns and substituting yarn, can be used for achieving a custom result.

Question 174:
Why did I use more yarn than it stated in the pattern?

No two people knit in exactly the same manner and, even though you are using the yarn stated in the pattern, and achieve the correct gauge, you could still find that you do not have quite enough yarn to finish the garment. Different dyes can alter the properties of a yarn; dark colors need more dye than light ones. This means that a ball of a dark color will have fewer yards to the ounce/gram than a ball of a lighter color. When you buy yarn, always check the ball bands for their weight and length.

If you alter your needle size to achieve the correct gauge this may also affect the amount of yarn you use. Also, any changes that you make to the pattern, a few extra rows, or a different stitch, will affect the quantities. If you plan to make any of these changes, buy an extra ball in case the store does not have the same dye lot when you return. If you substitute one yarn for a similar type but of a different brand, check the yardage on the ball band again. If you substitute with a completely different type of yarn, then you will need to estimate how much you will require by working a gauge swatch and measuring how much yarn it takes.

BELOW **Samples of yarn with information labels.**

Question 175:
How do I join in a new yarn?

Never knot the yarn in the middle of a row; the knot will always be noticeable, however neatly you try to do it, and will inevitably work its way to the right side of the garment! Join yarns at the side edges by tying them lightly together as you knit and then darning them in along the sides later, as described on page 124.

If you are working in the round, either join the yarn in the most unobtrusive position you can, such as where a side seam would be, and darn it in as above or use one of the following methods:

Splicing

Trim the old yarn to half its strands for 3 or 4 inches (8–10 cm); do the same with the new yarn. Place the two ends overlapping top to tail and twist them together. Moisten your fingers slightly and run them along the joined ends until you can feel that they won't pull apart. Knit carefully with the spliced yarn for the next row or two.

Folding

This is least noticeable on textured yarns or when using textured stitches, but it is not very effective with thick yarns since it will double their thickness at the join. When there are 3 or 4 inches (8–10 cm) of the old yarn left, fold the end of the new yarn around it close to the needles. Knit the next stitch with the old yarn and the following few stitches with the new doubled yarn. Darn the remaining ends in when the work is finished.

EXPERT TIP

66 You can make a decorative feature of your joined ends by working them on the right side in the middle of a row. Tie the ends into a bow and then add a few extra ones when the work is finished. **99**

Question 176:
How do I measure my gauge in a textured yarn?

Many of the modern yarns with long fibers, sometimes known as eyelash yarns, are very difficult to measure accurately in the normal way.

One method is to place a marker before and after the required number of stitches on the first row that you are using as your measuring point, and again on the last row. You will then have four markers forming a square. Measure the points between these markers. Because of the nature of the yarn it may be difficult to get a truly accurate measurement.

A second method is to note how many stitches you have cast on and how many rows you have worked, and then measure the finished size of the swatch. You will need to do a calculation to figure out if your piece will match the required gauge of the pattern.

These techniques also apply if you are working a very textured or lacy pattern. Work your swatch over a given number of repeats, since with these kinds of patterns this information is usually given in the instructions. If all of these methods fail, measure your swatch at different points, and if the measurements vary take an average reading.

BELOW A difficult-to-measure textured yarn.

Question 177:
What is a "schematic"?

A schematic is used more often nowadays, but at one time it was only found in some European patterns. It is a diagram, often stylized, of the finished shape of the pieces before they are joined and it contains all of the measurements that you are likely to need as you knit. As well as the measurements, a schematic often contains the number of stitches and rows required at each measuring point.

To be most helpful, these measurements should include not only the width and length of the body but also the depth and width of the neckline, the drop of the shoulder, and the length of the armhole. The sleeve measurements should include the width at the beginning and after the cuff, the width before the top of the sleeve is shaped, and the width of the head of the sleeve where appropriate, as well as the length of both sections of the sleeve.

A schematic is most useful when you are designing your own garments. Copy a blank one several times and then use your gauge swatches to work out the measurements and stitch/row counts for each new item. It can also be a useful tool for adapting an existing pattern, keeping to the same basic shape but altering the length or the neckline as you wish.

BELOW **Sample schematic.**

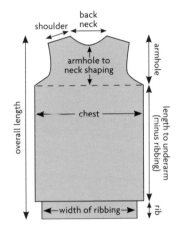

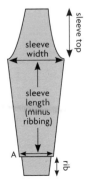

A = cuff width.

Question 178:
What do I do if I drop a stitch?

If the stitch has dropped down one or two rows in a column of knit stitches, insert the tip of the right needle from front to back into the stitch loop and catch the strand lying behind it, lift the strand through the loop and onto the right needle, again making sure that it is not twisted. Repeat this for the next row and replace the stitch onto the left-hand needle ready to knit. For a column of purl stitches, insert the tip of the right needle into the stitch loop from back to front and pick up the strand lying in front of it, drawing it backward and onto the needle. Alternate these actions if you are working garter stitch or a mixture of stitches.

If you drop a stitch in a lace pattern and you are not sure where you are in the pattern, replace it on the left-hand needle, and then undo back to the beginning of the row by slipping the left needle into the stitch of the row below and lifting the made stitch above it off the right-hand needle by pulling the yarn upward slightly. Repeat this back to the beginning of the row.

ABOVE **Picking up a dropped purl stitch.**

Question 179:
What do I do if I notice a dropped stitch several rows below?

Before the stitch drops any further, put a safety pin through it, then take a crochet hook a size or two smaller than the needles you are using. Insert the hook into the stitch as above, depending on what stitch you are using, remove the safety pin, and catch the first strand. This will automatically create a new stitch on the hook. Repeat the process until all the strands are lifted, then replace the stitch on the needle.

You may find that it becomes more difficult to lift a strand as you work upward. This is because you have continued knitting without leaving enough yarn to accommodate the missing stitch. But eventually these tight stitches will even themselves out, although you can help the process by gradually tightening the others along the row by pulling them one at a time with the tip your needle.

If you have dropped a stitch in a lace or textured pattern that will be complicated to pick up, hold it on a safety pin and then stitch it down as unobtrusively as possible when the work is finished.

Question 180:
How do I adapt an existing pattern?

If you have a pattern that you like but you want to make a few alterations to it, use the schematic if there is one, or draw up your own if there is not. Transfer it to graph paper, using one square for each stitch and mark this diagram with any changes that you wish to make.

Perhaps you want to alter a round neck to a V-shape. Sketch in the shape of your new neckline, beginning at the lowest point and ending at the shoulders. On the graph paper, follow the line, keeping those squares that the line passes through and stepping them in one square as the line moves beyond them. These will be the rows on which you decrease.

Similarly you can alter a short sleeve to a longer one by keeping the same number of stitches at the beginning of the sleeve head and drawing a line that indicates the length of your sleeve to its narrowest point just above the cuff. Mark the increases at the point where the line moves into the next square.

It is also possible to determine these figures by working out the number of stitches you need to decrease or increase and calculating which rows to perform the shapings on. For example, if you need to increase 16 stitches along the sleeve edge, that means you need to work an increase row eight times, assuming you are increasing at the beginning and end of each row. If you have 80 rows in which to perform these increases you will increase at each end of every tenth row.

Question 181:
If a pattern has complex instructions how do I turn it into a chart?

Many patterns, especially older ones, only give stitch-by-stitch instructions for texture or color work. This can be difficult to read accurately, especially when you first begin the pattern and a number of rows are very similar. It may seem time-consuming, but it is much easier to visualize the finished result if you chart the instructions first.

For color patterns, use paper with rectangles rather than squares to reflect the true ratio of stitch to row; or, if you use squared paper, allow for the design to look a little squashed. Use colored pencils or symbols to fill in the design. Most other designs can be charted on squared paper.

There are now universal symbols for knitting. A blank square usually denotes a knit stitch and a dot or dash denote a purl. Other symbols reflect the shape of the stitch, such

as, / for knit two together; \ for slip one, knit one, pass slipped stitch over. An "O" is useful for a yarn over in lace patterns. A symbol I use is a "V" with a number at its center for increase # stitches in one. I also use an upside-down "V" for a multiple decrease—but you may find it easier to follow some of your own. Cable patterns can also be charted with diagonal lines or symbols, such as ⌐ indicating the direction and numbers of stitches crossed.

If you are working a patterned garment with complex shaping, it can also be helpful to draw the piece on graph paper, marking each increase and decrease and indicating the position of the pattern if these shapings have changed it any way.

Question 182:
Is it possible to substitute a different yarn for the one quoted in the pattern?

Yes, it is possible to substitute yarns, but there are pitfalls. First of all, even if your yarn is meant to be the same type as the one in the pattern—for example, fingering or sportweight—it may not be exactly the same thickness. Many yarns give an indication of suggested needle size and gauge on the ball band, and this is a better indication than the name of the type of yarn. If the gauge is very different, then it is probably not sensible to use that particular yarn for that pattern. Try to find something that is a bit closer in match. You may need to change needles by one or two sizes, but this should not present a problem if you can get to within one stitch and row of the suggested gauge.

If your stitch count is near enough but the row count is out, check how much shaping you need to do per row. If your row count is too far out it is probably best not to risk using it unless you are prepared to refigure your calculations. The various pieces may not fit together correctly, especially where you are working a set-in sleeve and the instructions for the body were to work so many inches after the armhole shaping. The sleeve head will require a set number of rows to reduce the stitches, and this will not measure the same as your armhole. However, a drop sleeve pattern will have very little effect on the row count, and if there is not much shaping elsewhere then you should be able to use your substitute yarn.

ABOVE Both yarns are sportweight but the same size needles give more stitches to the inch with the green yarn than with the light blue yarn.

Question 183:
How do I know how much yarn I will need if I substitute?

There is no easy answer to this question. Depending on the fiber content, the quantities of yarn required could be very different. Check the number of yards to each ball as this is a better guide than the weight. Not all yarns indicate the length, so bear in mind that synthetics will usually have more yards to the ounce than wool, and that cotton, silk, and metallic yarns will probably have less.

Work a gauge swatch, as large as you are prepared to do, and then weigh it. Calculate how many of these swatches would fit into your finished piece and then work out how much yarn you will need for the whole. Allow a ball or two extra for bands, patterning, and so on.

Question 184:
If I notice a mistake a few rows down, how do I correct it?

If the mistake is not a very large one, work to the stitch above it on your current row and then drop that stitch and let it run down to the mistake. Correct the error and pick up the stitch with a crochet hook as described before.

A mistake over more than one stitch can also be corrected in this way, but it is safer to drop them one at a time, or put them onto a safety pin while each one is being picked up. An alternative to this is to slip the stitches onto a pair of double-pointed needles and reknit them using the strands that form the ladder.

If the mistake is a major one, it is probably better to unravel the knitting to that point and redo it. If you are taking the work off the needles, thread contrast yarn or a fine knitting needle through the row before the mistake. If unraveling and reknitting is too daunting, try using the method for lengthening a garment (see page 206) and then grafting the pieces together after the repair.

Question 185:
Is it possible to alter the size of a pattern?

If you like the style and shape of a pattern but it doesn't come in your size you can alter it by one or two sizes, so long as the stitch pattern is not too complicated and there is no unusually difficult shaping.

You will need the gauge given in the pattern and possibly some graph paper, although if the pattern is fairly simple you can probably work with the figures alone.

Read the number of stitches to the inch, and before going any further check whether the designer has allowed so much ease that one of the quoted sizes will actually fit you. If not, the next step is to add on (or subtract) the number of stitches you need to give you the correct width. If the garment contains a pattern stitch, check the number of stitches in the repeat and adjust your figures to accommodate this if necessary.

Next do the same for the row count, unless there is little or no shaping in the garment and the pattern simply says to work so many inches. If this is the case you can now go ahead and knit the back and front(s). When you reach the neck shaping, alter it by binding off more or less stitches according to your

calculations, and work the decreases for the number of times given in the pattern. You may need to count these if it is not actually stated. If you have shaped sleeves you will have to adjust the shaping at the armhole for the bound-off stitches, and probably in the head of the sleeve where you will need to work more or less rows between the decreases.

EXPERT TIP

“Where a pattern repeats over a large number of stitches and would make much too big a difference to the size, you may be able to work a half pattern at the beginning and end of each row instead. Chart it out on some graph paper first to make sure it will work.”

Question 186:
Can I alter the length of a garment after it is finished?

This is a handy tip, especially for children's clothes where the wearers grow taller but stay the same width! However, it only works successfully on stockinette or garter stitch because the stitches of the new portion will be half a stitch out on the older section.

First unpick the side seams for three or four rows above the hem or ribbing. Run a length of smooth thread (crochet cotton is ideal) through the stitches of the row just above the hem and two rows above this one. Cut the end stitches of the unmarked rows and pull out the yarn. Slip the stitches from the top marked row onto a knitting needle and knit downward for as long as you want.

Graft the stitches from this edge back onto those on the other thread, or undo the original hem and use this to continue knitting a new one. You may have to steam the crinkles out of this yarn first. If you do not have enough of the original yarn then knit a few rows of stripes, or knit a lacy edging with a different yarn.

If you plan ahead and you think you may want to alter the length of a garment at some stage, try knitting it all from the top down. It is then a simple matter to unpick the bind-off row and continue the knitting for as long as you want. And you won't have problems with the half stitch displacement!

LEFT The lower portion of the knitting is partially removed and ready to pick up "live" stitches.

RIGHT Skirt knitted from the top down.

MORE TECHNIQUES AND SOME FUN

13

Freeform, finger knitting, and working from the top down
—here are a few things to entertain you while helping you
learn even more about knitting as your proficiency improves.

Question 187:
What is "finger knitting"?

There are two kinds of finger knitting, one to make cords and the other just for fun.

The first method is said to have been used for making the cord or girdle for a monk's habit. For this you need two balls of yarn, one held in each hand.

Tie the yarns together and place the knot so formed in the palm of the right hand. Lift one of the yarns over the right index finger and hold the knot between your thumb and middle finger. Wrap the second yarn over your index finger in front of the loop and pass the loop over it. Slip the new loop onto the left index finger. Pull the first yarn to close the stitch. Repeat these actions alternating the fingers.

It is sometimes difficult to remember which finger you are on; use contrasting yarns as a reminder.

The second method of finger knitting is possibly one of the earliest known ways of linking loops of fiber. The yarn is wound in and out of the five digits of one hand and then back again. Where a strand passes above another, the strand below is lifted over it.

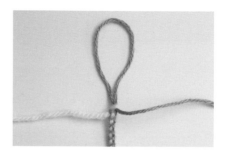

ABOVE Finger-knitted cord.

ABOVE Wrapping yarn around fingers.

ABOVE Lower strand being lifted over the one above.

Question 188:
How do I make a Dorset button?

The true Dorset button is one that is stitched, as follows:

Using a long thread and sewing needle, cover a metal ring with buttonhole stitch. Cover it closely and do not let any part of the ring show through. Turn the stitches inward so that the straight edges are on the inside of the ring. Using a second piece of thread, fasten it firmly to one of the edge stitches and then take it across the ring to the opposite side; pass it through the edge of the stitch and then bring the needle up through a stitch further along, across the ring, and down through the corresponding stitch on the other side. This will form a series of spokes that are then linked at the center with a cross stitch. The button is now finished, but it could be decorated further with more stitching or with beads.

It is also possible to make a similar button using a crochet hook. Work over the edge of the ring with single crochet, then work a few chain stitches to attach the yarn to the other side of the button. Work single crochet into the several stitches until you reach the halfway point. Work another set of chain stitches to link to the other side.

The centers of the crochet buttons can be left as a cross or filled with more spokes, as you wish.

RIGHT The two types of Dorset button.

Question 189:
How do I knit from the top down?

This method of knitting is useful if you think you might want to adjust the length of a garment. It is also a way of knitting when you are not sure if you will have enough yarn.

If you are following a pattern, begin at the back neck and cast on the number of stitches on each row for the shoulder where it instructs you to "bind off." Work downward to the point where the armhole shaping would have ended, and increase here for the number of times that the pattern says to decrease. Cast on the stitches for the underarm. Now work the rest of the body downward. Continue in this way, increasing where the instructions are to decrease, and vice versa. The front pieces can be picked up from the shoulder edges to avoid the need for stitching them together. If the sleeve has a straight top, the stitches for it can be picked up from the armhole edge, which will also avoid some sewing up.

If you are not sure how much yarn you will have for a garment, work as above until you reach the armhole cast-ons. Leave the stitches for the back on a stitch holder and work the front(s) to the same position. Leave these stitches on a holder, pick up the stitches for each sleeve, and work these to the length you want. Knit the cuffs and the neckband. Return to the stitches left on the holders and knit them onto a circular needle. Continue knitting downward until you run out of yarn.

EXPERT TIP

66 You can try things on as you knit if you work upside down! Start socks at the toes by working each side of the cast-on row, or begin a hat at the top by casting on two stitches on each of four needles then increasing until it is the required size. 99

More Techniques and Some Fun

Question 190:
How do I count rows?

If you are working a simple pattern then it is easier to count the rows from the back of stockinette just as you do on your gauge swatch. Count each ridge as one row. In garter stitch each ridge is two rows, plus an extra row if your last row on the right side is a smooth one. Multicolored patterns are also easy to count on the knitting, as you have the colors to guide you.

Where a pattern is complicated, involving several crossed stitches, or a complex lace design, it is helpful to use a row counter. These come in various forms and can either be slipped onto the end of the needle, which is not as practical if you are using circulars, or stand alone. Some of them can also be hung on a cord to go around your neck. Unfortunately, all of them require you to remember to advance the counter at the end of each row!

Question 191:
How do I knit backward?

Sometimes it is useful to be able to knit backward rather than turning the work, for instance, when you are working on a large piece, or making several bobbles across a row. This is the method I use.

Keep hold of the yarn in your usual way, at the back of the work. Insert the left-hand needle into the back of the stitch on the right-hand needle. Bring the yarn over the left-hand needle from back to front. Lift the stitch over this yarn to form the new stitch. Repeat for each stitch. It is also possible to purl backward in a similar way.

Insert the left-hand needle from the back to the front of the stitch. Take the yarn under the needle, over to the front, and back through the stitch on the right-hand needle.

It might seem a little clumsy at first, but you will soon speed up and find this a much quicker way of working when doing short row shaping or working bobbles.

Question 192:
How do I measure my knitting?

It is a good idea, and often saves time unraveling and reknitting, to measure your knitting as you work. When you have worked for several inches, lie the knitting flat on a firm surface; finish in the middle of a row if there are too many stitches for the work to spread out. Measure the width first, without stretching it, and then the length. If there is a schematic with the pattern, check these measurements against it. If there is no schematic there should be an indication of the finished width and length at the beginning of the

pattern. If all is well continue with your knitting until you reach the armhole shaping and measure again. Then measure again when you reach the neck shaping and the shoulders.

Always measure vertically when checking the length. Do not try to bend your ruler around the curve of the armhole, and do not measure the sloping edge of a sleeve, but lay the ruler in a straight line from the cuff edge to the row where the armhole shaping starts.

BELOW Sleeve and front of a V-neck sweater.

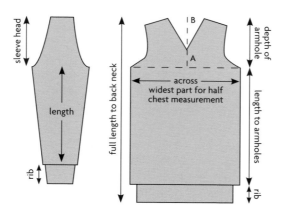

A = to start of neck shaping. B = depth of neck.
Measure all pieces vertically and horizontally.
Don't measure around a curve or along a shaped edge.

More Techniques and Some Fun

Question 193:
What is "freeform knitting"?

Freeform knitting, otherwise known as "scrumbling" is fun. You can use whatever yarn you like, mixing textures, weights, and fibers. After knitting your first shape, join on some other yarn and pick up as many stitches as you like from one of its edges. Knit another shape, make holes in it, or work some cables. Bind off and rejoin yarn somewhere else on one of these pieces. Continue adding shapes—large, small, plain, or fancy—as often as you like. Pull some of the pieces out of shape with hand stitching, or add buttons and beads or embroidery stitches.

You can use freeform knitting to create wall hangings as well as garments. Make a collage of torn paper to give you an idea of color and texture in your piece, or use a photo, illustration, or design for inspiration.

Strips of knitting of different textures can also be turned into wall hangings by weaving them in and out of one another, or stitching some of them side by side. Once you begin you will be inspired to make all kinds of things, and can try out some new stitch patterns at the same time.

BELOW **A piece of freeform knitting.**

Question 194:
What is "domino knitting"?

Domino knitting is a technique used for making squares that you join together without sewing. It is also a useful way of using up odds and ends of yarn. It works best in garter stitch, but a few rows of stockinette can be interspersed with it as long as this does not affect the frequency of the decreases or you adjust them to compensate. The squares can be any size but must be cast on with an odd number of stitches.

As you make more squares, work the first one as for the second one and the others as for the fourth one.

First square
Row 1 Cast on 41 stitches and knit 1 row.
Row 2 Knit 19, knit 3 together, knit 19.
Row 3 Knit.
Row 4 Knit 18, knit 3 together, knit 18.
Row 5 Knit.
Row 6 Continue like this, decreasing at the center of every alternate row until all the stitches are worked off. Change colors as often as you like.

Second square
Row 1 Cast on 20 stitches, then pick up 21 along the right edge of the first square. Complete as for first square.

Third square
Row 1 Pick up 21 stitches along the top of the first square, cast on 20. Complete as for first square.

Fourth square
Row 1 Pick up 20 stitches along the top of the second square, and 21 along the side of the third square. Complete as for first square.

Question 195:
What does "reverse shaping" mean?

This is an instruction often seen in patterns for cardigans, where the two fronts are worked as mirror images of each other. If a pattern instructs you to "work as for first piece, reversing all shapings," it means that you work any shapings at the other end of the row on the second piece. If you also want the shapings to match you will need to work a knit two together at the end where you worked a slip one, knit one, pass slipped stitch over at the beginning of the first piece to pair the decreases.

Armhole and neck stitches will need to be bound off on the right side of one piece and with the wrong side facing on the other piece in order for them to be worked at the correct edge.

It may be easier to work out where to place the shaping if you remember that your side seam will be on the right edge of the left front when you have the right side of the work facing you, and on the left side of the right front when the right side is facing you.

Question 196:
What do "RS" and "WS" mean?

These can also be confusing terms, since RS signifies right side—meaning the side that the designer, or yourself, wishes to be the outermost side of the garment. This is not to be confused with right front, meaning the side of a cardigan or vest that will be on your right-hand side when you wear it, but on your left as you look at it flat on a table, for instance.

WS signifies the wrong side according to the designer, and the shapings will have been worked out accordingly. However, there is no rule that says you cannot change this if you prefer the wrong side as your outermost side. The nice thing about knitting is that it is flexible, in both senses of the wordl

If you are working in the round, then the right side (RS) will always be facing you and the wrong side (WS) will be on the inside of the needles.

Question 197:
What is "double knitting"?

This term is confusing. It can either mean a particular type of yarn of a certain thickness, with the abbreviation DK; a yarn of worsted weight; or it can mean a way of knitting that creates a tube without the use of circular needles.

Double knitting can be worked in two different yarns or colors when one side will be made up of one color and the other side another color.

RIGHT Purse made using double (or tubular) knitting.

HOW IT'S DONE

Cast on an even number of stitches.

Row 1 * Knit 1, slip 1 purlwise with the yarn in front, repeat from * to end.
Row 2 Knit the slipped stitches and slip the knitted stitches in the same way as Row 1.
Row 3 And subsequent rows, as Row 2.

Question 198:
Why do some pattern instructions contain an asterisk?

You will see in many knitting patterns, including some in this book, that there is an asterisk at the beginning of a row. This is to signify that the portion of the pattern marked with the asterisk is to be repeated, either to the end of the row or as many times as instructed. Thus a pattern might say:

Row 1 * K1, p2, repeat from * to last stitch, k1.

This means that if the row were written out in full it would read:

Knit one, purl two, knit one, purl two, knit one, purl two, and so on, until you reach the last stitch, which you should knit.

Sometimes the instructions will contain asterisks at some point along the row, such as:

Row 1 K1, p2tog, * k1, yo, k2tog*; rep from * to * to last 3 sts, p2 tog, k1 .

This means:

After working the first knit one, purl two together, you continue repeating; knit one, yarn over, knit two together until you reach the last three stitches, then work purl two together and knit the last stitch.

EXPERT TIP

66 Use a highlighter pen to mark the portions between the asterisks if there are lots of pattern rows. This is especially useful where the asterisks are on different lines of the pattern or over a page. **99**

Question 199:
Why are some figures in parentheses?

Just as with asterisks, parentheses indicate a group of stitches. They will usually be followed by the number of times that you are to work those stitches. For example:

> * K6, (p2tog, yo, p2tog, k3) 3 times, k3; repeat from * to last stitch, k1.

Which in full means:

> Knit six, purl two together, yarn over, purl two together, knit three, purl two together, yarn over, purl two together, knit three, purl two together, yarn over, purl two together, knit three, knit three, then knit one at the end.

Parentheses are also used to group sizes where more than one is given for the pattern; the smallest size is usually given first followed by the others. For example:

> To fit sizes 24 (26, 28, 30)

In the body of the pattern, the numbers of stitches required for these different sizes will also be in parentheses in the same order. It is helpful where there is a large number of sizes to circle the one you are knitting throughout the pattern. And note that sometimes one or more of the sizes may be singled out for slightly different instructions, such as "second and fourth sizes only," increase 2 (4) evenly on the first row. This means that for the second size you would increase two stitches, and for the fourth size you would increase the number in the parentheses, in other words, four. No increasing is required for the other two sizes.

Always read through your pattern completely before starting to knit, and note anything that might trip you up later!

Question 200:
What is "smocking"?

Smocking is a form of embroidery on knitting. It will draw in the fabric and needs to be at least one-third again as wide as the rest of the garment. It looks best worked in light- to medium-weight yarns.

The stitches to be smocked are knitted in a rib pattern, usually one stitch knit and three to five in purl. If the rib were any wider than this the fabric would draw in too much.

When the work is the required depth, the smocking is worked over the knit stitches by backstitching.

Thread a blunt-ended sewing needle with a contrasting yarn and fasten it to the bottom right of the area to be smocked. Bring the needle through the fabric from back to front just to the left of the second knit stitch. Take it across to the first knit stitch and pull the stitches together. Work one or two more stitches in the same place. Take the needle across to the next pair of stitches and draw them together in the same way. When this row of smocking is finished work the next set over alternate pairs of knit stitches a few rows above.

Some of the stitches can be decorated with beads or other embroidery.

BELOW **Smocking worked on a purl five, knit one base.**

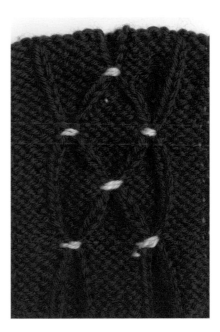

Useful Information

Abbreviations used in knitting instructions

Abbreviation	Meaning
alt	alternate; alternately
approx	approximately
B	bobble
beg	begin; beginning
BO	bind off
C	cable
CB	cable back
CF	cable front
ch	chain
Cc	contrast color
cm	centimeters
CO	cast on
cont	continue; continuing
cr	cross
dc	double crochet
dec	decrease
dpn	double-pointed needle
foll	following
G St	garter stitch
gms or g	grams
in(s)	inch(es)
inc	increase
incl	including
K	knit

Abbreviation	Meaning
ktbl	knit through back loop
k1b	knit 1 below
k2tog	knit 2 together
LHN	left-hand needle
MC	main color
M1	make one
MB	make bobble
mm	millimeters
oz	ounce
patt	pattern
psso	pass slipped stitch over
P	purl
rem	remaining
rep	repeat
rev	reverse
RHN	right-hand needle
RS	right side
sc	single crochet
sl	slip
St (s)	stitch(es)
St st	stockinette
tbl	through back loop
tog	together
tw	twist
WS	wrong side
yb	yarn back
yf	yarn forward
yo	yarn over
yrn	yarn round needle

Conversion table for needle sizes

Beginning at the top with the finest. The first six are usually only used for miniature knitting and are between 6 and 8 inches (15–20 cm) long.

U.S.	Metric	U.K.
8/0	0.5	24
6/0	0.75	22
5/0	1.00	19
4/0	1.25	18
000	1.5	17
00	1.75	15
0	2	14
1	2.25	13
-	2.5	-
2	2.75	12
-	3	11
3	3.25	10
4	3.5	10
5	3.75	9
6	4.00	8

U.S.	Metric	U.K.
7	4.5	7
8	5.00	6
9	5.5	5
10	6.00	4
10.5	6.5	3
-	7.0	2
-	7.5	1
11	8.00	0
13	9.00	00
15	10.00	000
17	12.00	0000
18	14.00	-
19	15.00	-
36	20.00	-
50	25.00	-

Terms used in knitting instructions

U.S. terms	UK terms
bind off	cast off
gauge	tension
Kitchener stitch	grafting
stockinette	stocking stitch
single crochet	double crochet
double crochet	treble crochet

Terms used to describe various weights of yarn

Recommended needle sizes (in millimeters)

U.S.	UK	Needle sizes
10 count crochet/bedspread	No. 10 crochet	various
bulky/super chunky	Chunky/bulky/big wool	8 mm and upward
chunky/bulky	chunky/bulky	5.5 mm – 8 mm
lace/light fingering	two-ply	1.5 mm – 2.25 mm
light/knitted worsted	DK-double knitting	3.75 mm – 4.5 mm
sock/fingering/baby	three-ply	2.25 mm – 3.25 mm
sport/fingering/baby	four-ply	3.25 mm – 3.75 mm
worsted/heavy worsted	Aran	4.5 mm – 5.5 mm

Index